Christmas Sermons

STERLING W. SILL

Christmas Sermons

STERLING W. SILL

Published by Deseret Book Company, Salt Lake City, Utah 1973

ISBN Number 0-87747-503-2
Library of Congress Number 73-86165

Lithographed by

DESERET PRESS

in the United States of America

CONTENTS

Christmas Sermons

O NE OF THE interesting characteristics of our lives is the wide variety of experiences of which they are made up. We have different kinds of work; the contrasts in our thoughts cover an extended area; and different occasions have different significance to us. Even the days of our week are different and are used for a different purpose. It has been said that our civilization itself would never have survived for half a century if it had not been for this one day in seven that we call Sunday.

This is the day that serves as our Sabbath. This is the day when we try to reach a pinnacle in our performance, This is the day when we pay particular attention to the cleanliness of our bodies and minds. This is the day when we put on our best clothes and think our best thoughts and read our best books. This is the day when we associate with the people that we love the most. This is the day for which we usually reserve the best meal of the week.

And then after we have laid aside the cares that usually concern us during the other six days, we go to the house of prayer and let our minds reach up and try to understand the purposes for which this day was set apart. We set aside one day to use for that important idea of thanksgiving; on one day we celebrate the Fourth of July; on one day we commemorate Easter; and one day we set apart as a day of memories, which we call Memorial Day. We set apart the second Sunday in May as Mother's Day and the third Sunday in June as Father's Day, in which we keep that great command, "Honor thy father and thy mother."

Then, in his great wisdom, God himself has set apart one-seventh of all the days as Sabbath days. This is a kind of Heavenly Father's day when we try to honor God by living at our best. We may let down our guard a little bit between Monday and Saturday, but by the time the Sabbath comes again, we try to get back up on the highest level where we can see the issues of life most clearly.

Then, once each year, we do something a little different. To give emphasis to this idea, we set aside a whole season as Christmas. This is a kind of Sabbath for the entire year. This is a whole season when we try to maintain ourselves at our highest level. This is also a time when we make an appraisal of the past and try to get ourselves ready for a brand new year. This is when we make our new year's resolutions, set our goals, and at our best we make some determinations of what our eternal lives should be like.

This recalls the idea that we also have different kinds of communications and instructions. Between ourselves, with each other, and with God, our speech itself has a different purpose. We have a type of conversation that is primarily intended as a means of killing time. Speech is also used to give instructions in geography or history. We sometimes tell each other how to be more effective in our occupations and our recreations. Even for our Sunday experiences or our Christmas communications, we have several kinds of verbal interchange. Our righteous prayers are carried to the throne of God.

One of our most important kinds of communication with each other is what we call the sermon. Sermons carry with them a little more serious tone than do mere conversations or stories of life's ordinary experiences. The dictionary says that a sermon is a serious address. It is made up of religious instruction. It may have to do more intimately with our conduct or our understanding or our duty or our sacred life's opportunities. A sermon is language dressed up in its best clothes. A sermon is usually grounded on some passage of scripture or based on some other sacred text or experience. Shakespeare mentions that there are sermons in stones, tongues in trees, books in running brooks, and good in everything. God preaches great sermons to us through the wonders of his universe, the wisdom of his all-important natural laws, and by means of godliness, which he has put into the lives of his offspring.

Of course, some of the greatest sermons in the world are those recorded in the Holy Scripture. They were inspired by the Lord and primarily they tell us about God's own ideas and activities. They also project the most advantageous program for our benefit. Once each year we unpack our boxes of tinsel and Christmas decorations to make our Christmas trees and our homes more beautiful. At this season of the year we also use special Christmas salutations and printed messages of peace and good will to each other. We have our Christmas feasts and enjoy our sparkling Christmas festivities. And then, in addition, we ought to unpack some great ideas so that with ourselves and our children we can read and hear and think and speak some Christmas sermons.

It is hoped that what follows may help us to dress up our spirits in their finest ambitions so that we may live at our best throughout the new year.

The Star of Bethlehem

ONE OF THE most important texts in the New Testament is found in the second chapter of Matthew, which reads as follows:

"Now when Jesus was born in Bethlehem of Judæa in the days of Herod the king, behold, there came wise men from the east to Jerusalem, Saying, Where is he that is born King of the Jews? for we have seen his star in the east, and are come to worship him." (Matthew 2:1-2.)

And that is what wise men have been doing ever since. Ever since that day when wise men from the East followed the star that led them to the manger in Bethlehem, other wise men have also been asking, "Where can we find Jesus? How can we know the Savior?" It is a small wonder that this should be so, for as Peter says, "Neither is there salvation in any other: for there is none other name under heaven given among men, whereby we must be saved." (Acts 4:12.)

The journey of the wise men was over when they had found the King, and so is ours. His life represents the main objective in our lives. In our own day the objective has been renewed and the Lord has said, ". . . seek me diligently and ye shall find me. . . ." (D&C 88:63.) Certainly the greatest tragedy of the world of 1900 years ago, as well as our own world, is found in the large number of people who fail to find the King. Jesus said, "He that seeketh me early shall find me. . . ." (D&C 88:83.) We fail to find only when we fail to seek. Certainly the greatest discovery ever made is when man discovers his Redeemer.

A great many people have found Jesus at this period of the year when we set aside a whole season in which we open our hearts to commemorate his birth. It is our custom at Christmastime to go back and relive those important events that began nearly twenty centuries ago when the angel Gabriel came from God to a virgin in Galilee named Mary and told her she would give birth to the Son of God. (Luke 1:35.)

Just before Jesus was born, a decree had gone out from Caesar Augustus that all the world should be taxed. (Luke 2:1.) And because everyone was required to go to his own city, Joseph took Mary and traveled from Nazareth in Galilee to Bethlehem of Judea. When they arrived, there was no room available in the inn, and so an improvised lodging was arranged for them in the stable, where Jesus was born.

The announcement of the birth was made by an angel to some shepherds who were tending their flocks upon the neighboring Judean hills. (See Luke 2:8-14.) It was also made in several other places to people living greater distances away from Bethlehem. Among these were the wise men from the East. I would like to present their story, which someone has written in verse.

The Three Kings

Three kings came riding from far away,
Melchior and Casper and Balthazar.
Three wise men of the East were they,
And they traveled by night, and they slept by day,
For their guide was a beautiful, wonderful star.

The star was so beautiful, large and clear
That all the other stars of the sky
Became a white mist in the atmosphere.
And by this they knew that the coming was near
Of the Prince foretold in the prophecy.

Three caskets they bore on their saddle bows,
Three caskets of gold with golden keys.
Their robes were of crimson, with rows
Of bells and pomegranates and furbelows,
Their turbans like blossoming almond trees.

And so the three kings rode into the west,
Through the dust of night, over hill and dell,
And sometimes they nodded with beard on breast,
And sometimes they talked, as they paused to rest,
With the people they met at some wayside well.

"Of the Child that is born," said Balthazar,
"Good people, we pray you, tell us the news.
For we, in the east, have seen his star,
And have ridden fast and have ridden far
To find and worship the King of the Jews."

But the people answered: "You ask in vain.
We know of no king but Herod the Great."
They thought of the wise men as men insane,
As they sped their camels across the plain,
Like riders in haste who could not wait.

And when they came to Jerusalem,
Herod the Great, who had heard this thing,
Sent for the wise men and questioned them;
And said, "Go down unto Bethlehem,
And then bring me tidings of this new king."

So they rode away; and the star stood still,
The only one in the gray of morn.
Yes, it stopped—it stood still of its own free will
Right over Bethlehem on the hill,
The city of David where Christ was born.

And the three kings rode through the gate and the guard
Through the silent street, till their camels turned
And slowed as they entered the great inn-yard;
But the windows were locked, and the doors were barred,
And only a light in the stable burned.

And cradled there on the scented hay,
In the air made sweet by the breath of kine,
The little Child in the manger lay,
The child that would be King one day
Of a kingdom, not human, but divine.

His mother, Mary of Nazareth,
Sat watching beside his place of rest,
Watching the even flow of His breath,
For the joy of life and the terror of death
Were mingled together in her breast.

They laid their offering at His feet;
The gold was their tribute to a king;
The frankincense, with its odor sweet,
Was for the priest, the paraclete;
The myrrh, for the body's burying.

And the mother wondered, and bowed her head,
And sat as still as a statue of stone;
Her heart was troubled, yet comforted,
Remembering what the angel had said
Of an endless reign of David's throne.

Then the kings rode out of the city gate,
With a tramp of hoofs in proud array,
But they went not back to Herod the Great,
For they knew his malice and feared his hate,
So they returned to their homes by another way.

Not only the wise men but the shepherds also went to see and worship the newborn King. Luke says of the shepherds, "And it came to pass, as the angels were gone away from them into heaven, the shepherds said one to another, Let us now go even unto Bethlehem, and see this thing which is come to pass, which the Lord hath made known unto us. And they came with haste, and found Mary, and Joseph, and the babe lying in a manger. And when they had seen it, they made known abroad the saying which was told them concerning this child. And all they that heard it wondered at those things which were told them by the shepherds. But Mary kept all these things, and pondered them in her heart. And the shepherds returned, glorifying and praising God for all the things that they had heard and seen, as it was told unto them." (Luke 2:15-20.)

What an interesting and important picture for us to contemplate at this Christmas season! We might ask for more information about this particular event. How many were present in this visiting company of the heavenly host who came praising God and singing, "Glory to God in the highest"? We might also ask who these visitors were.

We know that the word *angel* as used in the New Testament came from a Greek word meaning "messenger." Angels of God were, of course, messengers of God. We have learned a great deal about angels from latter-day revelation, which tells us that all of God's messengers to this earth are those who *do* belong or have belonged to it. (D&C 130:5, 129:1, 130:4-5, 130:67.) For example, we know that Gabriel was one of the great prophets who had lived upon this earth some 2,000 years before Christ. But all of that great multitude were children of God, and whether they had lived or were yet to live upon the earth, they were all dependent for their salvation upon the atonement of Christ. Some of us who are now living upon the earth may have been present that night on the Judean hills. Since the resurrection of Christ, some of God's messengers are resurrected personages who have bodies of flesh and bones just as Jesus has had since his resurrection. (D&C 129:13.) Of course, those who came to announce the birth of Christ had not yet had the privilege of resurrection, inasmuch as Christ was the first fruits.

We also might ask ourselves why the birth of this one baby was so important as to call forth this great celebration even in heaven? In order to get a full answer, we need to go back behind the scenes. The birth of Christ had been ordained in the grand council of heaven; it had also been foretold many generations before it actually took place in Bethlehem. Some 700 years B.C. the prophet Isaiah gave a partial account of a vision that he had had of that antemortal council. It had to do with the time when the First Begotten Son of God in the spirit was being chosen as the Savior of what was as yet an unborn race of mortals. He was ordained to redeem a world yet in its formative stages of development.

Isaiah said, "Also I heard the voice of the Lord, saying, Whom shall I send, and who will go for us?" (Isaiah 6:8.) Modern revelation tells us that there were two who responded. One was the First Begotten Son of God in the spirit who was particularly qualified for this special mission. He answered and said, "Here am I, send me. . . . Father, thy will be done, and the glory be thine forever." (Moses 4:1-2.)

Another also spoke. It was Lucifer, the brilliant son of the morning. And he said, "Behold, here am I, send me, I will be thy son, and I will redeem all mankind, that one soul shall not be lost, and surely I will do it; wherefore give me thine honor." (Moses 4:1; see also D&C 76:27; Isaiah 14:12-14.)

Here we see initiated these two opposing philosophies, which have continued with us ever since. The First Begotten Son of God offered to come to the earth in the interests of our redemption. Lucifer offered to come in the interests of his own glory. God said, "I will send the first." And the record says that "the second was angry, and kept not his first estate." (Abraham 3:27-28.) Because Lucifer did not get his own way to serve his own interests, he became rebellious, and ever since he has fought against the work of God. Lucifer was cast out of heaven and one-third of the hosts of heaven were cast out with him. They became fallen and were deprived of the privilege that all of us who did not follow Lucifer receive, that of mortal life upon this earth.

In the preexistence Jesus was known as Jehovah and was a personage of great power. He was associated with Elohim, his Father, in the creation of the world. Just before his death Jesus said in his prayer to his Father, "I have glorified thee on earth: I have finished the work which thou gavest me to do. And now, O Father, glorify thou me with thine own self with the glory which I had with thee before the world was." (John 17:4-5.)

Jesus came to the earth under the commission from God and the council of heaven to redeem the world and save us from death on condition of our repentance. The song says:

> There was no other good enough
> To pay the price of sin.
> He only could unlock the gates
> Of heaven and let us in.
> —*Hymns,* no. 201

But those who had lived upon the earth and those who would yet live upon the earth had an equal interest in the mission of the Savior. Jesus broke the bonds of death and initiated the resurrection. He also serves as the pattern for us to follow.

In foretelling the life of Jesus, Isaiah said, "For unto us a child is born, unto us a son is given: and the government shall be upon his shoulder: and his name shall be called Wonderful, Counseller, The mighty God, The everlasting Father, The Prince of Peace." (Isaiah 9:6.) Someone has suggested that we remove one comma so that the line would read, "and his name shall be called 'Wounderful Counsellor.' " Our lives depend on following his counsel. He was a wonderful counselor in the preexistence, and he has been a wonderful counselor here. We need to follow that counsel more closely.

May God, our Heavenly Father, who by the shining of a star did guide the eastern wise men to behold his Son and our Redeemer, may he by the light of his inspiration guide us to find and follow the Savior of the world. And as the wise men of old laid at his feet gold and frankincense and myrrh, may we present the offering of a humble heart, an adoring spirit, and an obedient will.

No Room in the Inn

EACH YEAR at Christmastime our minds go to a pilgrimage back to the little town of Bethlehem, which has nestled among the Judean hills for so many centuries. The name Bethlehem means the house of bread, which might lend itself to more than one interpretation. Certainly it is wonderfully rich in its long and interesting history. It was here that Jacob buried his wife Rachel. Bethlehem is where Ruth gleaned in the wheat fields of Boaz. It was also here that Ruth's great-grandson David was born and where he tended the sheep of his father, Jesse. It was here that he was anointed by Samuel to be the king of Israel. This little town finally called itself by the name of its most famous son and was thereafter known as the City of David.

The Old Testament prophet Micah had foretold that one greater than David should also be born in Bethlehem and that the most important event in the history of the world should here take place to distinguish little Bethlehem above all of the great cities of the world. Since the meridian of time, Bethlehem has been remembered primarily as the birthplace of the Savior of men.

For that first Christmas, Mary and Joseph had come some 65 miles from Nazareth in Galilee to Bethlehem in Judea in response to the decree of Caesar Augustus that all the world should be taxed, each in his own city. They arrived in Bethlehem at about the time that Jesus was to be born. And Luke says of Mary, "And she brought forth her firstborn son, and wrapped him in swaddling clothes, and laid him in a manger; because there was no room for them in the inn." (Luke 2:7.)

As we think back to the birth of Jesus, we feel a certain sense of shame and regret that there was no room in the inn for the Savior of the world to be born. It is also a very interesting thought that the King of kings and Lord of lords should be born in a stable. With his Heavenly Father, he had created the earth in the first place, and yet there was no room in it for him to be born. But this fact is something more than an isolated event of interesting significance; it indicates what almost amounts to a theme song for his life. "No room" was one of the chief characteristics of his entire mortal existence. He himself summed up his experiences by saying, "The foxes have holes, and the birds of the air have nests; but the Son of man hath not where to lay his head." (Matthew 8:20.)

He was not very old before the fierce opposition of Herod was directed against him. As soon as Herod learned of his birth from the wise men, he sent soldiers to Bethlehem to kill the children. Judea was not big enough for a peaceful coexistence of both Herod and Jesus, so while Herod remained in power, Joseph and Mary took Jesus into far away Egypt because there was "no room" for him in the domain of Herod. After Herod's death others kept the antagonism going as they continued to cry, "No room, no room." There was "no room" for his teaching, "no room" for his doctrine, "no room" for his miracles. The chief priests and religious leaders wanted him put to death because they saw in him the downfall of their religious system, and there was "no room" for both. Some argued that he was a threat to the Roman world. Even in his death there was no place for his final rest, and so Joseph of Arimathea took his body from the cross and laid it in his own tomb.

The birth and death of Jesus are now both ancient history. Since those historic events, some nineteen centuries have come and gone. The great Roman Empire has long since become little more than a memory. The problems of the religious leaders who brought about his death have long been buried with their dust. But Jesus did not give his life for his contemporaries alone; his mission applied with equal significance to us. It was our sins as well as theirs that made him volunteer his own death. What is our attitude about his life?

We now delight to identify ourselves with the great name of Christian, and well we might. We have everything that others have had to convince us of his divinity. In addition, we have the judgment of time shining upon the life of Christ. We have the solemn assurance of the ancient apostles who sealed their testimony with their blood, bearing witness to us that he was divine. On top of that, we have a great flood of testimony from many new witnesses.

The question now before us is, What have we done about it? We have greatly increased our standard of living. There are very few persons who would not now account it an unendurable hardship to have to live as Solomon lived in all of his glory. We have lengthened our own life expectancy from approximately nineteen years, as it was in Jerusalem in the days of Jesus, to seventy years. We have vastly expanded our educational opportunities and our material accomplishments. We have cut in half the number of work hours required to earn our living. We have multiplied our luxury and increased our leisure time, but what spiritual advantage have we received from our superior education and the extra time placed at our disposal?

Certainly the peace that the angels sang about has never seemed farther away than now. The great nations are crouching, ready to spring at each other with their hands filled with weapons too horrible to think about. The sin and evil that Jesus came to free us from is in many places now running unchecked through the world. Crime is at its awful height. Jesus came as our example. He lived a sinless life and furnished us with a working model of righteousness. His message was "Follow me." He asked us to follow him in his doctrine, to follow him in his righteousness, to follow him in his love for others. But we have not followed Jesus; rather we have followed those who could find "no room." "No room" is still the significant cry of our world. We have made room for his gifts but we have found no room for the giver. We have made room for the extra leisure time, we have made room for our physical comforts, we have made room for horse races and baseball games, we have made room for many violations of the Sabbath day, but we have no room for worship, no room for service, no room for the Savior of the world. Instead, every day we reproduce in our lives that ancient scene at Bethlehem.

The fact that there was no room for him to be born in the inn is not nearly so significant as that there is no room for his way of life. We have not taken seriously the prayer of the angels singing "Glory to God in the highest." We plan to put peace in force with atomic bombs, while we continue to reenact that historic drama of Bethlehem over and over again, not just in the pageants that we present at Christmastime, but this is what is also presented upon the greater stages of our individual lives. It has been said that souls are not saved in bundles or bunches.

Salvation is an individual matter, and Jesus approaches each of us with the offer of personal exaltation. His most important message has always been strictly individual, and today as of old, Jesus is saying to us, "Behold, I stand at the door, and knock: if any man hear my voice, and open the door, I will come in to him, and will sup with him, and he with me. To him that overcometh will I grant to sit with me in my throne, even as I also overcame, and am set down with my Father in his throne." (Rev. 3:20-21.)

Many of the doors with which Jesus was familiar had the latch only on the inside and could not be opened from without. The door to the heart is still opened from within. The invitation for Jesus to enter our lives must still come from the inside. The door of the heart is not easily broken down by anyone beating upon it from without; the release must be operated from within.

At Christmastime it is wonderful to sing:

> O Holy Child of Bethlehem,
> Descend to us we pray,
> Cast out our sin and enter in,
> Be born in us today.

> We hear the Christmas angels
> The great glad tidings tell,
> Oh, come to us, abide with us,
> Our Lord Emmanuel.

But even though we sing the most beautiful songs and even though he stands at the door of our lives and knocks, not many doors are being opened. Too frequently we merely send back the ancient reply, "No room, no room."

There was no room in Bethlehem because all of the available space was occupied. That still remains one of our most vexing situations. There are thousands of people who presently can find no room for Jesus because their lives are so completely filled with the pursuit of material things that they have little time for anything else. Making money so occupies our thoughts that we sometimes don't even recognize our needs. Then, like the Laodiceans, we think, "I am rich and increased with goods and have need of nothing." The Laodiceans did not even know that they were "wretched and miserable and poor and blind and naked."

Some of us have no room because our lives are so filled with ignorance that understanding can find no place to set its foot. Others have no room for Jesus because their lives are so heavily loaded with sin. Some have hearts filled with sloth and have no room for the efforts required by salvation. You can't pour more water into a vessel that is already overflowing. Some have no time—no time to worship, no time for meditation, no time to get acquainted with his teachings, no time to feed our hearts on the things of the spirit, no time to devote to our own souls and to the God who created us. Our time is all taken up, and our activities are already fully allotted. Someone has said:

> No time for God, what fools we are,
> To clutter up our lives with common things
> And leave without the Lord of life and life itself.
>
> No time for God, as well to say,
> No time to eat, to sleep, to live, to die;
> Take time for God or a poor misshapen thing you'll be
> To step into eternity and say to him,
> I had no time for thee.

Today Jesus stands at the citadel of our souls pleading for entrance. He pleads through the spoken word. He pleads through the scriptures. He pleads through the Spirit. He pleads through the voice of reason. He pleads through the witness of faithful parents and friends. But because we have no space left, we reply, "No room, no room." We have no room for Jesus because most of us are looking for a religion of convenience, one that takes no time, costs no money, requires no effort, and will fit our lives without any changes on our part.

As the spirit of Christmas fills our lives and as we are haunted by our embarrassment from nineteen centuries past, we should consider the advisability of making room for him in our own present. If we are too busy to serve God, we are much too busy. If our lives are so filled as to crowd him out, then we should empty our lives and relieve the congestion that threatens to overthrow us. If the bucket of our lives is overloaded with dross, how are we going to be able to find some way to make room for some pure gold?

In readjusting his life, one man once made up a long list of those things that he could get along without. That is a pretty good idea for our eternal success. Some of our lives are too full of sin. Some of us could get along with a little less ignorance and a little less indifference. Maybe we should pour out some of our interest in nonconstructive things to make room for the things of God.

There is a famous painting entitled "Christ Before Pilate." Some day we may see another picture entitled "Pilate Before Christ." There may also be some future picture of some of us being turned away from celestial glory because there is no room there for lives overflowing with the wrong things. It is interesting to remember that all of these things that monopolize our interest and keep us from God will also keep God from us. And all of these we had better learn to get along without.

There is a sacred song that says, "I walked today where Jesus walked." And wouldn't it be a thrilling thing if we could go and stand on that very spot of ground where Jesus stood and try to absorb the spirit of his life. Or suppose we go into Gethsemane and kneel at that place where under the burden of our sins he sweat great drops of blood at every pore and there try to recapture the spirit of his life. Or suppose that we go in imagination and stand before the final judgment. Then we might be able to more easily make up that interesting list of things that our lives could profitably get along without.

It may not be practical for us to walk today where Jesus walked. But it *is* practical and a lot more important to think today what Jesus thought. We can live today as Jesus lived. We can unload our hearts of evil and clear the lethargy out of our ambition. Then we can fill our minds with our Father's purpose and our hearts with an understanding of his ways. We can loosen the latch and open the door of our souls and make room for the king of glory to come in. To make room for our Redeemer is the greatest opportunity of our lives. Jesus is still saying as in olden times, "Behold, I stand at the door, and knock: if any man hear my voice, and open the door, I will come in to him, and will sup with him, and he with me. To him that overcometh will I grant to sit with me in my throne, even as I also overcame, and am set down with my Father in his throne." (Acts 3:20-21.)

My Christmas wish is that we may change that ancient Christmas pageant of Bethlehem so that we may really hear the angels' song and make room for the Redeemer of the world in our personal lives.

Dickens' Christmas Carol

ONE OF THE finest authors of our world was Charles Dickens, who lived over a hundred years ago. And to this date he is regarded by many as the greatest English novelist of all time. He wrote fifteen great novels, including *The Pickwick Papers, Oliver Twist, David Copperfield, A Tale of Two Cities,* and *Great Expectations.* He possessed a generous abundance of creative energy. He was a sheer genius as a storyteller and has an exuberant style that sweeps his readers along in a wonderful journey of delight. His great masterpiece *A Christmas Carol* was written in 1843. It is said to be the most famous Christmas story in the world and perhaps the best-known short story in the entire English language. It is repeated many times each Christmas on television. However, in spite of its great popularity, there are many people who still have not read nor heard nor seen it—nor are they familiar with the great lessons that it teaches.

The chief character in this story is a selfish, stingy, money-grubbing, money-squeezing old man by the name of Ebenezer Scrooge. Scrooge had a lot of bad attitudes. He had some bad attitudes about life, and he had some particularly bad attitudes about Christmas. Then one evening at Christmastime, after he had locked himself into his dingy rooms for the night, he had what was probably the greatest experience of his life. He received a visit from the spirit of his dead business partner, whose name was Jacob Marley.

During his lifetime Marley had been a man of similar tastes and tendencies to those of Scrooge himself. Marley had died seven years before, on this very night. The ghost of Jacob Marley announced his presence by a loud clattering noise on the floor below, and he came banging up the stairs dragging behind him a long line of fetters, money boxes, etc. In answer to his partner's question, Marley's ghost said, "These are the chains I forged in life." Jacob was bemoaning that human blindness which allows some mortals to live their lives and pass on into eternity without ever discovering that life is too short for selfishness and the ignorance that sometimes cause us to fail to discover that no amount of future regrets can make amends for missed opportunities. Scrooge tried to soften his former partner's lament by saying to him, "But you were always a good man of business, Jacob."

Then, wringing his hands in anguish, the ghost cried out, "Business, business, mankind was my business! The common welfare was my business! Charity, mercy, forbearance, benevolence were all my business!"

However, in this main business of their lives, both Scrooge and Marley had miserably failed. But Marley was still trying to help, and he said to his former partner, "Hear me! My time is nearly gone. I am here tonight to warn you that you have yet a chance and hope of escaping my fate." And then Marley explained to Scrooge that his one hope consisted in the possibility that Scrooge might yet learn some of those important lessons of life before it was too late. The ghost gave Scrooge the startling information that he was about to be haunted by three ghosts. One was the Ghost of Christmas Past; the second was the Ghost of Christmas Present; and the third would be the Ghost of Christmas Yet to Come.

This might remind us of the experience of Saul of Tarsus, who also had some bad attitudes about the One whose birth we celebrate at Christmastime. And Saul was not only visited; he was stricken down on the Damascus road, and after he had changed his attitude he was given another chance to mend his ways.

Scrooge was informed that he was to expect the first spirit just after midnight. The others would come in turn. As Marley's allotted time had now run out, he walked backward and disappeared out of the window. After this exhausting experience, Scrooge fell on his bed without undressing and immediately fell into a deep sleep.

He was awakened by the clock tolling its deep, dull, hollow, melancholy sound of one o'clock. Some unusual lights flashed up in Scrooge's room, and at that very instant the curtains of Scrooge's bed were drawn aside by a strange, unearthly figure. This Ghost of Christmas Past was like a child and yet it had some of the features of an old man. As Scrooge viewed the specter, the Ghost announced himself as the Spirit of Christmas Past. He was the spirit of Scrooge's own past. The spirit said to Scrooge, "Arise and walk with me." Because Scrooge seemed to have no choice, he stood up and together they walked back through time while they visited some of the places of Scrooge's happier life during his youth.

This ability to relive the past reminds us of the old mythical deity Janus, who was the Roman god of January. An interesting thing about Janus was that he had two faces. With one he looked back into the past while he studied his mistakes. With the other face he looked up into the future so as to eliminate its possible errors. During this visit back into his own past, Scrooge was allowed to relive some of his earlier Christmases where he felt again some of the joys and thrills of his childhood. This was before he had acquired his present bad attitudes and habits.

During this interesting experience, Scrooge relearned some of those important lessons of love, loyalty, and happiness that every child ought to feel at least during this holy period of Christmastime. However, Scrooge also felt great unpleasantness and unhappiness as he relived the shadows of those events that had already taken place. As he felt the disloyalty and failure in his present situation, he begged the spirit to take away these unpleasant memories and remove him from his present surroundings. Scrooge said, "I cannot bear it. Believe me, take me back, haunt me no longer." And as he struggled with his own soul, he discovered that he was again in his own bedroom. By exhaustion and an irrepressible drowsiness, he barely had time to reel over onto the bed before he again sank into a heavy slumber.

The next time that Scrooge was visited, he was awakened by the great lights of the second ghost, who announced himself as the Ghost of Christmas Present. Scrooge said to him, "Spirit, conduct me where you will. I went forth last night on compulsion and I learned a lesson which is now working in my soul. Tonight if you have aught to teach me, let me profit by it."

The spirit said, "Touch my robe." Scrooge did as he was told and held it fast. The room and its contents all vanished instantly and they stood in the city streets upon a snowy Christmas morning. Scrooge and the ghost were invisible and the Ghost took him straight to the home of Bob Cratchit, who was Scrooge's loyal clerk. On the threshold of the door, the spirit smiled and stopped to bless Bob Cratchit's humble dwelling place. Then Scrooge was permitted to witness some of the thrills and delights that were in the hearts of the members of Bob Cratchit's family as they kept Christmas the way it should be kept.

Scrooge marveled at the spirit of the little crippled boy, Tiny Tim, who rode mostly upon his father's shoulders. Scrooge was greatly impressed with the prayers that were said, the love that was circulated, and the happiness that was enjoyed in that humble home as they ate and played and danced and worshiped and sang their Christmas together. To the Cratchits, Christmas was a long way from what Scrooge had called it—a humbug. And because Scrooge was not visible, he heard them discuss what they thought of Scrooge and his unpleasant point of view about life and so many other things.

One of the important parts of Dickens' great Christmas story centers in this idea of the ability to intimately inspect the lives of people when they are living at their best. It is like standing before a lighted house at night when the shades are all undrawn so that you can see into every corner of human life. Suppose that we might stand with the ghost and the invisible Scrooge and look into the depths of human souls and hear their opinions about us. It might also be of great help to have an intimate viewing of how the Cratchit family kept Christmas and hear the prayer of each member, including Tiny Tim, who prayed from his heart and said, "God bless us, every one!" Then we might try to appraise the effect of such an experience upon the selfish, stingy, hardened heart of Scrooge, or of ourselves.

Finally the time came for Scrooge to be approached by the third ghost, which was the Ghost of Christmas Yet to Come. He said to the ghost, "I fear you more than either of the other specters I have seen, But as I know your purpose is to do me good, and as I hope to live to be another man from what I was, I am prepared to bear you company and do it with a thankful heart." And he said to the spirit, "Lead on."

This ability to see the future is one that God has also given to many people. Some of the prophets have looked thousands of years into the future. For example, some nineteen hundred years ago, John the Revelator was shown the final judgment exactly as it will someday be. But we can also learn to look ahead and see the consequences of our deeds. H. G. Wells wrote an interesting fantasy that has a foundation in truth. He entitled it *The Time*

Machine. In this time machine he could go back into the past and see any of the important events of the past as they were actually happening. Then he could push the lever of the time machine in the other direction and go up into the future and see things as they would sometime actually take place.

I have a relative who does something similar. When she reads a novel, she always reads the last chapter first. She wants to know before she begins where she is going to be when she gets through. And that is a pretty good idea for life.

So the Spirit of Christmas Yet to Come took Scrooge up into his own future. Among other things, the spirit showed him what his own death would be like if he continued as he was. Scrooge saw himself as he was dying, alone and unattended. Because of the selfish way in which he had lived, he then had no friends and no one to mourn for him. The spirit showed him a neglected grave with his name written on the stone. He was shown many other unpleasant things that would happen if changes were not made. Scrooge begged the spirit to assure him that if Scrooge changed his ways, the result would also be changed. Then Scrooge said to the spirit, "I am not the man I was. I will not be the man I would have been but for the experiences of this night." Scrooge said, "I will honor Christmas in my heart and try to keep it all through the year. I will not shut out the lessons that Christmas teaches." And Scrooge held up his hands as one engaged in prayer, asking God to enable him to reverse his own fate.

When Scrooge awakened, he was in his own bed. He heard the church bells ringing out their Christmas music. He ran to the window and put out his head to find out for sure what day it was. In his experience with the spirits he had lost track of time, and when he was told that it was Christmas morning, he was delighted. He was still alive, and with his changed attitude he could make up for all of the problems of his past.

As it was said of someone else, so it was thereafter true of Scrooge that he went around doing good. Scrooge soon learned how to keep Christmas, and so great was his joy that he had a kind of Christmas every day. How much better everyone looked to him now! How much more happy he himself was! Scrooge had made a great discovery. He had discovered that the most pleasant and the most profitable activity comes from righteousness and

Christlike service to other people. Therefore he served out the balance of his life living the spirit of Tiny Tim, who said, "God bless us, every one." And may God help us to get the greatest good from our great Christmas experience

The Prince of Peace

THIS IS THE period of the year when we commemorate the birth of the greatest life that was ever lived. The most important considerations of our individual existence center in him who is known to us as Jesus Christ. Next to the Father himself, the Son was, and is, the greatest intelligence in the universe. He was commissioned to be the Savior of the world and to redeem all men from death upon condition of repentance. He lived the perfect life and established the pattern for us to follow.

The most important general force in our lives is often the uplifting effect that others may have upon us. Certainly there are very few undertakings more profitable than to study the biographies of great men and women. As we become familiar with the best traits in the lives of others, we naturally appropriate their ideas and adapt their virtues for our own use. This borrowing process achieves its highest significance at this particular season of the year. It is at Christmastime that we most effectively hold up before our minds the great virtues and noble characteristics of the greatest Man who ever lived.

We think of greatness partly in terms of what it has already accomplished and partly in terms of what it promises for the future. We might most profitably begin our Christmas consideration of the life of the Master by a mental excursion back into his preexistence.

Jesus was the first begotten Son of God in the spirit. Paul refers to him as the "firstborn among many brethren." (Romans 8:29.) And he was chosen to be the Savior of the world because he was the best qualified for that important responsibility.

It was decided in the council of heaven that this preeminent Son of God should come into the world, and take upon himself our sins, and do the other necessary things for us that we could not do for ourselves.

Over seven centuries B.C. the prophet Isaiah foretold the birth of Christ. We are all aware of the significance that a name or a title may have in describing an important office. Isaiah uses the wonderful titles of Savior and Redeemer. He refers to him as "Mighty God, the Everlasting Father." (Isaiah 9:6.) It was by his intelligence and power that worlds were organized and their laws and order established. This magnificent personage is known in the Old Testament as Jehovah, the God of Abraham, Isaac, and Jacob. Isaiah also calls him "Wonderful," "Counseller." How appropriate it would be to move the comma and call him a Wonderful Counselor.

From the time of Adam to our own day one of his primary duties has been to give us counsel as to how we might eventually become even as God is. To follow his counsel would guarantee our eternal glory in the celestial order to which the Father and the Son themselves belong. Jesus said that he came that we might have life and have it more abundantly.

Finally he was placed on trial, not only for his life but also for his way of life. Yet just think how the lives of everyone would be transformed if we actually followed his pattern. Suppose that we followed the counsel that he gave from the top of Mount Sinai, when out of the fire and smoke, accompanied by the lightnings and thunders of that holy mountain, Jehovah gave those ten great commandments. Or think what quality would be given to our lives if we actually lived the Sermon on the Mount or obeyed the stimulating revelations of the latter days. Just suppose that the Golden Rule, the Word of Wisdom, and God's marriage covenant were fully applied to our individual lives. Then suppose that we made ourselves familiar with every other truth that he has given and anxiously put into actual operation his high standards of honor, integrity, and righteousness.

There is no one to whom we owe a greater debt than to him whose birth we commemorate at this particular season. Not only were we created in God's image, but each of us has been endowed with a set of his attributes and potentialities. One of his most stimulating titles and one that is of particular interest to our present world is the one where Isaiah calls him "The Prince of Peace." And Isaiah said of the increase of his government and peace there shall be no end. What a thrilling hope for a war-weary, sin-laden world!

Seven hundred years after Isaiah had spoken these words, a great concourse of angels came to the earth to announce Christ's birth and reproclaim his title. As we space travel, we are more than ordinarily awed by the fact that at this early day such a multitude of the heavenly host came from such a distance for this all-important occasion. Since that day, over nineteen centuries have come and gone, and yet the angelic promise of peace on earth, good will toward men has never yet been realized. In fact, it has seemed that the very opposite has been true. Rather than peace, these nineteen centuries have been filled with apostasy, frustrations, evil, disbelief, and war. And certainly no age can compare in strife and unrest with the present day. Some of the most prominent and powerful men in the world are devoting themselves to keeping the people in a state of constant turmoil and unrest.

The editors of *U. S. News and World Report* once commented on the troublemaking propensities of a prominent Communist dictator. They pointed out how he causes one crisis after another. Certainly he will create a great many more trouble spots in the future. They pointed to him as a persistent troublemaker with no other apparent purpose than to cause contention, unpleasantness, and misery. And while every honest person condemns his trickery and duplicity, yet there are many people who in their daily lives are more inclined to follow him than Christ. There are few of us indeed who excel as peacemakers and follow the one ordained of God to be the Prince of Peace.

When the Savior visited the early inhabitants of the Western hemisphere, he tried to make their lives more successful by saying, "There shall be no disputations among you as there have hitherto been." He said, ". . . he that hath the spirit of contention is not of me, but is of the devil, who is the father of contention, and he stirreth up the hearts of men to contend with anger, one with another." (3 Nephi 11:29.)

And while under Satan the Communist dictator operates upon a broad international stage, some of us may also be guilty in our more limited spheres. Sin always destroys peace, and frequently through our unrighteousness we sow the seeds of disagreement and unhappiness. The individual and the home are the most common seats of strife and bitterness among people. And there can never be peace and good will in lives or in homes where sin flourishes. For a very good reason, no sin is ever tolerated in the presence of God. Neither should it be tolerated in our presence and certainly not in our conduct.

A young mother recently had a nervous breakdown because of the deceit, irresponsibility, and unrighteousness in her husband. He seemed to match on a personal basis the duplicity and troublemaking abilities of the dictator. He made a hell for his wife and children, whereas kindness and consideration for others are among the greatest Christian virtues. And this was one of the virtues always practiced by the Prince of Peace, even upon the cross.

Recently I reread *The Life of Mohandas K. Gandhi,* by Louis Fischer. Although Gandhi was not a Christian, he was often described as one of the most Christlike of men, and his chief characteristic was peace. Almost single handed he won the independence of India entirely by nonviolent means. He would tolerate no falsehood or threat of force in himself or in any of his followers. He would far rather suffer wrong than do wrong. His motive was happiness for others even though they made him suffer pain or imprisonment. Then on that fateful evening of January 30, 1948, as he was walking to the prayer ground for his evening devotion, he was shot by a crazed fanatic. Gandhi lived just long enough to forgive his assassin and pronounce a blessing upon him.

Nineteen hundred years earlier from the top of Mount Calvary, Jesus has said of his own assassins, "Father, forgive them; for they know not what they do." (Luke 23:34.) Jesus earned the right to be called the Prince of Peace because he taught and lived the gospel of peace. Actually living the principles of peace is the only way that peace can be brought to the individual heart or to the world in general. Gandhi's last act before dying was to raise his hands and bless his assassin. During the entire life of Jesus, his mission was to bless people, and one of his main beatitudes was "Blessed are the peacemakers: for they shall be called the children of God." (Matthew 5:9.) What a thrilling title to which we ourselves may aspire. And what a thrilling example for us to follow.

What an inspiring season is Christmas, and what a great thrill it would be to really be a Christian. What an unexcelled opportunity we have to serve the Prince of Peace in our nation, in the church, in our homes, and in our own individual lives.

Because we do not all understand the real significance of Christmas, it comes to mean different things to different people. We have the child's Christmas. Its symbol is the toy, and its chief characteristic is excitement. Then there is the world's Christmas. Its symbol is the Christmas tree, and its chief characteristic is festivity. There is the drunkard's Christmas. Its symbol is the bottle, and its chief characteristic is sin. Then there is the Christian's Christmas. Its symbol is the star, and the chief characteristics are worship, righteousness, peace, and good will.

At this Christmastime, and at the more than 1900 other Christmastimes, all of the people of the earth have been searching for peace. And many and devious have been the methods by which they have attempted to bring it about. Some have thought to secure it by means of peace pacts; some have tried to secure it by drinking themselves into unconsciousness. But peace cannot be had by compact. It cannot be bought. It cannot be obtained by intoxication. It is so difficult to tremble and not to err. It is so hard to hit the mark with a shaking hand and a bleary eye. Peace can never be attained apart from righteousness.

The best way to get peace is by a personal obedience to the Prince of Peace. The crowning perfection of any good Christian is a clear conscience. With a good program of understanding and a righteous personal devotion, there arises in the soul a serenity and peace far surpassing the most satisfying bodily pleasures. Peace and good will are among the most pleasant of earthly delights. Fortunately, the poor can obtain peace as easily as the rich, the social outcasts gets it as freely as the leader of society, and the humblest citizen can have a peace equal to those who wield the greatest political power.

Jesus has offered us a peace that surpasseth understanding. He said: "Peace I leave with you, my peace I give unto you: not as the world giveth, give I unto you. Let not your heart be troubled: neither let it be afraid." (Matthew 14:27.) ". . . ye believe in God, believe also in me. In my Father's house are many mansions: if it were not so, I would have told you. I go to prepare a place for you . . . that where I am, there ye may be also." (John 14:1-3.)

This peace can only come through our fairness, righteousness, and truth. Emerson said, "Nothing can bring us peace but a triumph of principles." And we should always remember that the greatest principles that can triumph in any life are the principles of the gospel. They constitute the program of the Prince of Peace, who is also the prince of possibilities and the prince of glory and the prince of eternal progress.

I close with the salutation of the early Christians, "May the God of peace be with you all." (Romans 15:33.) "Peace be . . . to thine house, and peace be unto all that thou hast." (1 Samuel 25:6.)

Mind the Light

IN NEW YORK harbor between Manhattan and Staten Island is a sunken shoal called Robin's Reef. A small lighthouse stands there to warn of hidden dangers to those who go by sea. For many years the keeper of the Robin's Reef lighthouse was a woman, an elderly widow, by the name of Mrs. Jacob Walker. Mrs. Walker was once interviewed by some newspaper men. She told them the story of her life. It is a story of inspiration and devotion that shines out like the beams of the beacon she has so long minded.

She said: "I was a young girl living at Sandy Hook, New Jersey, when I first met Jacob Walker. He was the keeper of the Sandy Hook lighthouse. He took me there as his bride and we were very happy. Some years later we were transferred to the lighthouse at Robin's Reef. After four years my husband caught a cold while tending the light. The cold turned to pneumonia and they took him to a hospital on Staten Island. I remained behind to look after the light. A few nights later I saw a rowboat coming through the darkness. Something told me the message it was bringing. We buried my husband two days later on the hillside of Staten Island not too far away to be seen from the lighthouse. Every morning since then when the sun comes up, I stand at the porthole and look out across the water toward Jacob's grave. Sometimes the hill is green, sometimes it is brown, sometimes it is white with snow. But I always get a message from him. It is the same thing I heard him say more often than anything else in life. It is always the same, just three words: 'Mind the light.' "

That is a very short message, but it has an important meaning. The significance of its message is in some ways comparable to that other three-word message wherein Jesus said, "Come, follow me." Or it might be compared to the message that comes down to us from the morning of creation when God himself spoke a four-word command, saying, "Let there be light." With each new rising of the sun we might try to imagine what it must have been like to feel the oppression of that brooding, unbroken, unrelenting pre-creation darkness, and then picture to ourselves the contrast when in the forward march of progress God first said, "Let there be light."

Ever since that first day of creation so long ago, darkness in one form or another has continued to be the central problem of the world. In the beginning, "God saw that it was good" (Genesis 1:18), and God divided "the day from the night" (Moses 2:14), and he turned the faces of men toward the light.

But men have often turned about and have loved darkness rather than light. In Dickens' *Christmas Carol,* Scrooge, the central figure, sat in the darkness of his money-changing countinghouse and said, "Darkness is cheap; therefore I like it." But Scrooge was mistaken. Darkness has never been cheap. Darkness is the most expensive thing in the world—the one commodity that is always in the greatest and most constant oversupply.

With awful meaning, Isaiah looked down across the centuries to our day and said, "For behold, the darkness shall cover the earth, and gross darkness the people." (Isaiah 60:2.) The darkness that covers the minds of men is oppressive and stifling. We feel its offensiveness in the words of the Lord's fateful pronouncement about our own day, "And the whole world lieth in sin, and groaneth under darkness. . . ." (D&C 84:49.)

It is one of the most startling and thought-provoking paradoxes of our day of wonders and enlightenment that men are still walking in darkness at noonday. (D&C 95:6.) Thus we bring upon ourselves the fate mentioned by John the Beloved, who said, ". . . if a man walk in the night, he stumbleth, because there is no light in him." (John 11:10.)

As disturbing as the darkness itself may be, it is still more disturbing to try to look behind the scenes and understand the reasons for the blackout that we bring upon ourselves. No less an authority than the Master himself has said that men "love darkness rather than light, because their deeds are evil." (D&C 10:21.) Some receive not the light because they perceive it not. (D&C 45:29.) They not only lack vision; they also lack interest. We sometimes voluntarily turn our faces the other way, even though we know that that which doth not edify is not of God but of darkness. (D&C 50:23.)

The one supreme gift that the inhabitants of our world need more than any other is the gift of light. The one line in all of sacred literature that should most concern us is the one wherein God said, "Let there be light." That is not only our greatest need; it is also his fondest wish for his children.

In various periods of the history of our world a renewal of that edict has been given, bringing light again into a darkened world. Speaking of this renewal in our own time, the Lord said, "And when the times of the Gentiles is come in, a light shall break forth among them that sit in darkness, and it shall be the fulness of my gospel." (D&C 45:28.) And God will judge all men according to the use they make of the light that is available. (D&C 82:3.) God has made it abundantly clear that the rejection of light is the greatest of all sins, and those who have great light and knowledge "and altogether turneth therefrom, shall not have forgiveness in this world nor in the world to come." (D&C 84:41.) It naturally follows that the greatest opportunity provided for man in this world is to join with creation in the program of bringing about God's first and probably most important decree of "Let there be light."

The bounds of darkness must be pushed back. The lighted frontiers must be extended in breadth and increased in intensity. The need of the world for more light "minders" and more light "carriers" is very great. Mrs. Jacob Walker spent her life directing the saving beams of her lighthouse beacons out across the dark waters of Robin's Reef. She was always faithful to her trust. She could always be depended upon. Each morning as the sun came up and God's day was renewed in the world, she stood at her post by the porthole and received her charge anew, "Mind the light."

Those who "mind the light" must always have foremost in their hearts the interests of others. Mrs. Walker translated that interest into service as the shafts of light reached out across the dark waters to bring safety to those who sailed within reach of the hazards of Robin's Reef.

The philosophy of light has always been one of the most important philosophies of our world. For behind the light there is God and goodness and safety and happiness for man. God is "the life and light of the world, your Redeemer, your Lord and your

God." (D&C 10:70.) It is he who enlighteneth every man that
cometh into the world that harkeneth to the voice of the spirit.
(D&C 84:46.) He is in the sun and the light of the sun and the
power thereof by which it was made. (D&C 88:7.) It is that light
that "enlighteneth your eyes . . . [and] quickeneth your understandings, Which light proceedeth forth from the presence of
God to fill the immensity of space—The light which is in all
things, . . . which is the law by which all things are governed,
even the power of God. . . ." (D&C 88:11.)

The same light that draws the stars across the sky pumps
your blood and activates your brain. It lights the shoals of
Robin's Reef and inspires the faithfulness of Mrs. Jacob Walker.
It enlightens every man in the things of God. It offers the greatest employment in the universe, which is to be "minders" and
"bearers" of light.

The duty of light bearers is to "chase darkness from among
men." (D&C 50:25.) The greatest need of men is greater light.
Just before his death, Bill Porter, known to many as O. Henry,
said, "Pull up the shades. I don't want to go home in the dark."
O. Henry concluded his life's story in a New York hospital with
this challenging statement, which might well be the burden of
the cry of church leadership. The last phrase spoken by Goethe
was, "More light." That is the life work of leaders and teachers.
The best way to have more light is to see that our own lives are
always increasing in brightness. The Lord has said, ". . . he that
receiveth light, and continueth in God, receiveth more light; and
that light groweth brighter and brighter until the perfect day."
(D&C 50:24.) "And every man whose spirit receiveth not the light
is under condemnation." (D&C 93:32.)

The spirit lived in light before it came here. Not to recognize
it and love it here may mean "outer darkness" hereafter. Our entrance into this world is as a reward of faithfulness in our former
state, and our position in the world to come is now being de-
termined by how we mind the light that we have been given.

To be an effective "minder," one must himself have a quality of spiritual phosphorescence. We must not only be reflectors,
but our own souls must be aglow from the depths inside of us. We
need to keep a light in our eyes and a light in our minds. We must
have lighted and enlightened souls. Jesus said, "Let your light so

shine before men that they may see your good works, and glorify your Father which is in heaven." (Matthew 5:16.)

Sometimes the light flickers uncertainly in our human lives. When we waver in our duty, the light grows dim. The Lord said, "If you keep not my commandments, the love of the Father shall not continue with you, therefore you shall walk in darkness." (D&C 95:12.)

Jesus was the chief light-giver of the world. He lights our lives and sends us out to light others. We are both givers and receivers of light.

> I met a stranger in the night
> Whose lamp had ceased to shine.
> I paused and let him light
> His lamp from mine.
>
> A tempest sprang up later on
> And blew the world about,
> And when the wind was gone,
> My light was out.
>
> Then back again the stranger came;
> His light was glowing fine.
> He held again the precious flame
> And lighted mine.

Our light does not grow less even if it kindles the flame for thousands. It was said that the light of an unknown continent burned within Columbus. The light of the eternal continent burns within us, and we must not hide it under a bushel. Jesus bids us put our light high on a candlestick that it may serve as the beacon for everyone to see. The Lord has established his own lighthouses and selected lighthouse keepers to "mind the light" and send it out to those who walk in darkness and danger.

> There's a call comes ringing o'er the restless wave,
> Send the light. Send the light.
> There are souls to rescue, there are souls to save,
> Send the light. Send the light.
>
> We have heard the Macedonian call today,
> Send the light. Send the light.
> And the golden offering at the cross we lay,
> Send the light. Send the light.

Let us pray that grace may everywhere abound,
Send the light. Send the light.
And a Christ-like spirit everywhere be found;
Send the light. Send the light.

Let us now grow weary in the work of love,
Send the light. Send the light.
Let us gather jewels for a crown above,
Send the light. Send the light.

Send the light, the blessed gospel light,
Let it shine from shore to shore;
Send the light and let its radiant beam
Light the world forever more.

Those who radiate light also generate warmth. Warmth is a manifestation of light. The two greatest of all the commandments have to do with warmth in human hearts. The warmth we radiate to others will also light their lives.

Tyndale, sitting in his cold dungeon prison, asked that warm clothing be sent him, "For," said he, "these I have are very thin." Then he asked for a lighted lamp and a Bible. Said he, "It is so dreary sitting alone in the dark."

How dreary might it be sitting alone in the darkness of eternity. Now is the time to get our lamps lighted and with our Bible begin our journey toward the city of eternal light. And each day for a brief period we might pause and stand at our own portholes while we receive anew from God our charge, "Mind the light."

The Other Wise Man

E ACH YEAR at Christmastime we de- light to follow the wise men as they came out of the East and made their way to Bethlehem, where they worshiped the newborn king and laid their treasures at his feet. Henry Van Dyke has told us about another wise man who also followed the star not only to Bethlehem, but through- out his life, and yet he never found the king. The other wise man's name was Artaban. He was a kind of unknown soldier who didn't quite make the headlines. He was also one of the magi and lived in Persia. He was a man of great wealth, great learning, and great faith. With his learned companions he had searched the scrip- tures as to the time that the Savior should be born. They knew that a new star would appear, and it was agreed between them that Artaban would watch from Persia and the others would ob- serve the sky from Babylon.

On the night that the sign was to be given, Artaban was speaking to nine of his magi friends in his home. He said to them, "My three brethren are watching at the ancient temple of the Seven Spheres, at Borsippa, in Babylon, and I am watching here. If the star appears, they will wait for me ten days, then we will all set out together for Jersualem. I believe the sign will come tonight. I have made ready for the journey by selling all of my possessions and have brought these three jewels—a sapphire, a ruby, and a pearl—I intend to present them as my tribute to the king." He said, "I invite you to make this pilgrimage with us that we may worship the newborn king together."

While he was speaking he thrust his hand into the inmost fold of his girdle and drew out three great gems—one blue as a ragment of the night sky, one redder than a ray of the sunrise, and one as pure as the peak of a snow mountain at twilight. He would give them all to the king. Then one of Artaban's friends said, "Artaban, this is a vain dream. No king will ever rise from the broken race of Israel. He who looks for him is a chaser of shadows." And he bid Artaban farewell and left his dwelling.

Each in turn offered his own particular excuse, and finally only his oldest and truest friend remained. He said, "Artaban, I am too old for this quest, but my heart goes with thee." Then with a hand on Artaban's shoulder he said, "Those who would see wonderful things must often be willing to travel alone."

Left to himself, Artaban put his jewels back into his girdle. Then he parted the curtains and went out onto the roof to again take up his vigil to watch the night sky.

As Jupiter and Saturn rolled together like drops of lambent flame about to blend into one, an azure spark was born out of the darkness beneath them, rounding itself with purple splendor into a crimson sphere.

Artaban bowed his head. "It is the sign," he said. "The king is coming, and I will go to meet him."

All night long Vasda, the swiftest of Artaban's horses, had been waiting saddled and bridled in her stall, pawing the ground impatiently and shaking her bit as if she shared the eagerness of her master's purpose.

As Artaban placed himself upon her back, he said, "God bless us both, and keep our feet from falling and our souls from death."

Under his encouragement, each day his faithful horse measured off the allotted proportion of the distance, and by nightfall of the tenth day, they approached the outskirts of Babylon. In a little island of desert palm trees Vasda scented difficulty and slackened her pace. Then she gave a quick breath of anxiety and stood stock-still quivering every muscle.

Artaban dismounted. The dim starlight revealed the form of a man lying in the roadway. His humble dress and haggard face showed him to be one of the poor Hebrew exiles who still dwelt in Babylon. His pallid skin bore the mark of the deadly fever that ravished the marshlands of Babylon at this season of the year. The chill of death was in his lean hand. As Artaban turned to go, a sigh came from the sick man's lips, and the brown bony fingers closed convulsively upon his robe.

Artaban felt sorry that he could not stay to minister to this dying stranger, but this was the hour toward which his entire life had been directed. He could not forfeit the reward of his years of study and faith to do a single deed of human mercy. But then, how could he leave his fellow man alone to die?

"God of truth and mercy," prayed Artaban, "direct me in the holy path of wisdom which only thou knowest." Then he knew that he could not go on. The magi were physicians as well as astronomers. He took off his robe and began his work of healing. Several hours later the patient regained consciousness.

Then Artaban gave him all he had left of bread and wine. He left a potion of healing herbs and instructions for his care.

Though Artaban rode with the greatest haste the rest of the way, it was after dawn when he arrived at the designated meeting place. His friends were nowhere to be seen. Finally his eyes caught a piece of parchment arranged to attract his attention. He caught it up and read. It said, "We have waited till past the midnight, and can delay no longer. We go to find the king. Follow us across the desert."

Artaban sat down upon the ground in despair and covered his face with his hands. "How can I cross the desert," said he, "with no food and with a spent horse? I must return to Babylon, sell my sapphire, and buy a train of camels and provisions for the journey. I may never overtake my friends. Only God the merciful knows whether or not I shall lose my purpose because I tarried to show mercy."

Several days later, when Artaban's train arrived at Bethlehem, the streets were deserted. It was rumored that Herod was sending soldiers, presumably to enforce some new tax, and the men had taken their flocks and herds back into the hills beyond his reach.

The door of one dwelling was open, and Artaban could hear a mother singing a lullaby to her child. He entered and introduced himself. The woman told him that it was now the third day since the three wise men had appeared in Bethlehem. They had found Joseph and Mary and the young child and had laid their gifts at his feet. Then they had disappeared as mysteriously as they had come. Joseph had taken his wife and babe that same night and had secretly fled. It was whispered that they were going far away into Egypt.

As Artaban listened, the baby reached up its dimpled hand and touched his cheek and smiled. His heart warmed at the touch. Then suddenly outside there arose a wild confusion of sounds. Women were shrieking. Then a desperate cry said, "The soldiers of Herod are killing the children."

Artaban went to the doorway. A band of soldiers came hurrying down the street with dripping swords and bloody hands. The captain approached the door to thrust Artaban aside, but Artaban did not stir. His face was as calm as though he were still watching the stars. Finally his outstretched hand revealed the giant ruby. He said, "I am waiting to give this jewel to the prudent captain who will go on his way and leave this house alone."

The captain, amazed at the splendor of the gem, took it and said to his men, "March on, there are no children here."

Then Artaban prayed, "Oh, God, forgive me my sin. I have spent for *man* that which was meant for God. Shall I ever be worthy to see the face of the king?"

But the voice of the woman, weeping for joy in the shadows behind him, said softly, "Because thou hast saved the life of my little one, may the Lord bless thee and keep thee; the Lord make his face to shine upon thee and be gracious unto thee; the Lord lift up his countenance upon thee and give thee peace."

Then Artaban, still looking for the king, went on into Egypt, seeking everywhere for traces of the little family that had fled before him from Bethlehem. For many years we follow Artaban in his search. We see him at the pyramids. We see him in an obscure house in Alexandria, taking counsel with a Hebrew rabbi who told him to seek the king not among the rich but among the poor. Then we follow him from place to place. He passed through countries where famine lay heavy upon the land and the poor were crying for bread. He made his dwelling in plague-stricken cities where the sick were languishing in the bitter companionship of helpless misery. He visited the oppressed and the afflicted in the gloom of subterranean prisons. He searched the crowded wretchedness of slave markets. Though he found no one to worship, he found many to serve. As the years passed he fed the hungry, clothed the naked, healed the sick, and comforted the captive.

Once we see Artaban for a moment as he stood alone at sunrise, waiting at the gate of a Roman prison. He had taken from its secret restingplace in his bosom the last of his jewels that he was saving for the king. Shifting gleams of azure and rose trembled upon its surface. It seemed to have absorbed some of the colors of the lost sapphire and ruby, just as a noble life draws into itself its profound purpose, so that all that has helped it is transfused into its very essence; the pearl had become more precious because it had long been carried close to the warmth of a beating human heart.

Thirty-three years had now passed away since Artaban began his search, and he was still a pilgrim. His hair was now white as snow. He knew his life's end was near, but he was still desperate with hope that he would find the king. He had come for the last time to Jerusalem.

It was the season of the Passover, and the city was thronged with strangers. There was a singular agitation visible in the multitude. A secret human tide was sweeping them toward the Damascus gate.

Artaban inquired where they were going. One answered, "We are going to the execution on Golgotha, outside the city walls. Two robbers are to be crucified, and with them another called Jesus of Nazareth, a man who has done many wonderful works among the people. But the priests and elders have said that he must die because he claims to be the Son of God. Pilate sent him to the cross, because he said that *he* was the 'King of the Jews.'"

How strangely these familiar words fell upon the tired heart of Artaban. They had led him for a lifetime over land and sea. And now they came to him darkly and mysteriously like a message of despair. The king had been *denied* and cast out. He was now about to perish. Perhaps he was already dying. Could he be the same for whom the star had appeared thirty-three long years ago?

Artaban's heart beat loudly within him. He thought, "The ways of God are stranger than the thoughts of men, and it may be that I shall yet find the king and be able to ransom him from death by giving my treasure to his enemies."

But as Artaban started toward Calvary, he saw a troop of Macedonian soldiers coming down the street, dragging a sobbing young woman with torn dress and disheveled hair. As Artaban paused, she broke away from her tormentors and threw herself at his feet, her arms clasping around his knees.

"Have pity on me," she cried, "and save me, for the sake of the God of purity. My father was also of the magi but he is dead, and I am to be sold as a slave to pay his debts."

Artaban trembled as he again felt the old conflict arising in his soul. It was the same that he had experienced in the palm grove of Babylon and in the cottage at Bethlehem. Twice the gift which he had consecrated to the king had been drawn from his hand to the service of humanity. Would he now fail again? One thing was clear—he must rescue this helpless child from evil.

He took the pearl from his bosom. Never had it seemed so luminous, so radiant, so full of tender, living luster. He laid it in the hand of the slave and said, "Daughter, this is thy ransom. It is the last of my treasures which I had hoped to keep for the king."

While he yet spoke, the darkness of the sky thickened and the shuddering tremors of an earthquake ran through the ground.

The houses rocked. The soldiers fled in terror. Artaban sank beside a protecting wall. What had he to fear? What had he to hope for? He had given away the last remnant of his tribute to the king. The quest was over, and he had failed. What else mattered? As one lingering pulsation of the earthquake quivered beneath him, a heavy tile, shaken from a roof, fell and struck him on the temple. He lay breathless and pale. The rescued girl leaned over him, fearing that he was dead. Then there came a still, small voice through the twilight. It was like distant music. The notes were clear, but the girl could not understand the words.

Then the lips of Artaban began to move, as if in answer, and she heard him say, "Not so, my Lord: For when saw I thee hungered, and fed thee? Or thirsty, and gave thee drink? When saw I thee a stranger, and took thee in? Or naked, and clothed thee? When saw I thee sick or in prison, and came unto thee? Thirty-three years have I looked for thee; but I have never seen thy face, nor ministered unto thee, my king."

As he ceased, the sweet voice came again. And again the maid heard it, very faintly and far away. But now she understood the words which said, "Verily, I say unto thee, that inasmuch as thou hast done it unto one of the least of these my brethren, thou hast done it unto me."

A calm radiance of wonder and joy lighted the face of Artaban as one long, last breath exhaled gently from his lips. His journey was ended. His treasures were accepted. The Other Wise Man had found the King.

The Yule Log

WE HAVE MANY delightful customs that center in the Christmas season. We send each other Christmas cards and vocally express our messages of good will. We decorate our homes with holly and colored lights. We set up a Christmas tree in the living room, hang up our stockings, and give and receive the presents of Christmas. But probably our most exciting custom is that of promoting in ourselves the Christmas attitudes. We relive the traditions of happiness and cheerfulness. And we enshrine in our hearts the stimulating ideals of Christmas. At this season we not only make our homes more beautiful, but we also put a little extra magnificence into our own lives by getting the Christmas spirit and filling ourselves with generosity and friendliness. Even our best *religious* impulses reach a high point as once a year we undergo this annual transformation that lifts our lives above the commonplace.

It is a part of the activities of the unusual season that in our minds we make a pilgrimage to Bethlehem, that we might be on hand to worship the newborn King. We watch the radiant Bethlehem star as it comes out of eastern skies, bringing a new significance to us and to all of mankind. With great joy we follow the wise men across the desert and join with them in laying our treasures at the feet of him who was born to be the Savior of the world. We not only sing the stimulating Christmas carols; as we relive that first Christmas, we join with the angels in their anthems of "Glory to God in the highest, and on earth peace, good will toward men." (Luke 2:14.)

Another interesting custom for this unusual season centers in the Christmas fire. This is best represented by the old Scottish tradition of the yule log. The Scots habitually prepared a large log to put on the hearth on Christmas Eve as the foundation of their traditional Christmas fire. Considerable care was taken in the log's selection. It was cut and drawn from the forest with great ceremony. As it passed along the way toward its destination, each wayfarer raised his hat, because it was believed that the yule log contained some wonderful promises for the future.

This sturdy yule log may have been growing in the forest for a hundred years, and during all of that long period it had been faithfully storing up within itself the energy and sunshine that it received from the sun. It was also believed that many excellent spirits living in the trees of the forest were released by the fire. Then, at just the right time, when everything was in readiness, the yule log was ceremoniously placed in position and set ablaze as the high point of the Christmas Eve festivities. And as it burned, it released a hundred years of stored-up warmth and strength into human hearts. The spirits of goodness and happiness that had so long been imprisoned in the yule log were also released to brighten the lives surrounding this particular fireside.

Civilization itself had its beginning around an open fire. In the earliest times, the family group gathered in the fire's light and warmth to find safety, strength, comfort, cheer, and companionship. If we trace the origin of our word *fireplace,* we find that it is related to a Latin word meaning "to focus." The home serves as the focal point in the lives of its members. It is the very center of our small, intimate, personal world. Home is not merely a residence place for the body. It is a sacred sanctuary in which children are welcomed into the world, a holy place in which we worship God and try to get the gospel of Christ in actual operation in our lives. Home is also the axis of the heart, a place of intimate companionship, where affections are developed, where children learn obedience to parents and love for each other. Home is where all members of the family learn to plan and toil harmoniously together in order to make life the kind of joyful blessing it was intended to be.

Then, for contrast, if one desired in one word to picture the most severe depths of want and unhappiness, he might describe one who was homeless. One of the most devastating of the negative emotions at Christmastime would be to imagine that we ourselves had no home and no one to love us, that we had no place to rest, that we had no place to go for Christmas. Often we refer to life as a hard-fought battle or a difficult journey. Actually, in one way everyone is a kind of pilgrim, and we are all on a pilgrimage. But no matter how far our wanderings may take us, we always try to get home for Christmas. When distant places have lost their enchantment and the ardor of our foreign adventures has cooled, when danger has been bravely faced and overcome and our wonder has been satisfied, then our hearts long for a resting place, which can only be found in the ruddy glow of the hearth fires of home.

In John Howard Payne's great musical masterpiece "Home Sweet Home," he says, "A charm from the sky seems to hallow us there." The right kind of home not only hallows our lives in this life, but it also helps to prepare us for that heavenly home hereafter that will be characterized by even greater magnificence and happiness. In one of his most significant messages, Jesus said, "In my Father's house are many mansions: if it were not so, I would have told you. I go to prepare a place for you . . . that where I am, there ye may be also." (John 14:2-3.) The primary reason for the birth in Bethlehem was that the Son of God might help us to prepare for our life hereafter. Because this life is a prelude and a preparation for the next, we might well expect the two to be similar. We know that God personally established the family here, and he has ordained that it should also be the basic unit throughout eternity. If it is unpleasant to be without a family and have no home to go to on Christmas here, how much more serious the problem becomes when eternity is involved.

What a terrible situation we tend to bring upon ourselves when, in our man-made marriage ordinances establishing the family here, we make a commitment that says "until death do us part." In this we are enacting a bill of divorcement as well as making a marriage covenant. Someone has said, "I desire no future that will break the sacred ties of the past." Christ was born to be the Savior of the world, and much of our salvation is built upon the family relationship. The education, spiritual unity, and righteous solidarity within the family circle are more than ordinarily significant, and in token of this unity we see a happy family gathered around a real Christian Christmas fire.

Several things are particularly fitting about this interesting yule log custom. For centuries we have used the figure of fire to describe some of our most important personality qualities. We describe an energetic, wide-awake, enthusiastic kind of person by saying, "He is on fire," or we call him "a fireball," or "a ball of fire." Or we say something about his "burning desire to accomplish," or he may even be "setting the world on fire." Certainly no one ever accomplishes much in any endeavor before he gets an elevated temperature and an increased pulse rate.

Fire also serves us as the symbol of God himself. The scripture says that "God is a consuming fire." But fire is more than a symbol of God. To give the Israelites their law, God came down onto the top of Mount Sinai enveloped in fire, and he went before them toward their promised land in a pillar of fire. In speaking of the second coming of Christ, the scripture says, ". . . the Lord Jesus shall be revealed from heaven with his mighty angels, in flaming fire taking vengeance on them that know not God, and that obey not the gospel of our Lord Jesus Christ." (2 Thessalonians 1:7-9.) The scripture says that God himself dwells in "everlasting burnings." John the Baptist announced the first coming of the Lord by saying that he would baptize his followers with the Holy Ghost and with fire. (Matthew 3:11.) The Holy Spirit is a kind of purifying agent for our lives. And God has referred to himself as a refiner's fire. His Spirit burns the dross from our hearts and refines our spiritual ambitions and attitudes. It is a part of his program that all of his children should be born of water and purified by fire.

An interesting word that is closely related in meaning to this idea is *enthusiasm.* This word is also sometimes used to express the burning qualities in the personality. The word *enthusiasm* itself came from the Greek words *en* and *theos,* which actually mean "God in us." They denote a kind of "divine inspiration," that is, when we get some of God's fire inside of us. To say that one is enthusiastic is just another way of saying that he has caught fire. It is probable that genuine enthusiasm adds as much real power to the personality as any other quality. Usually when people are charged with enthusiasm they have a light in their eyes, their faces are aglow, their friendliness is warm, their best impulses have a feverish eagerness to accomplish. Enthusiasm is often the fuel that keeps us going. The comparison has been made that men, like automobiles, go forward by a series of internal explosions.

The Christmas fire might also symbolize this important trait of "God in us." The fire that the tree receives from the sun is released into our lives and homes at Christmastime. It also provides the atmosphere in which the fires of faith may be most effectively lighted in our own lives. As we absorb the warm sunshine of love and happiness at Christmas, we become better than we were. This divine enthusiasm, this "God in us," is a virtue that is not only highly contagious; it is also transferable to others.

The Art of
Keeping Christmas

How can we best keep Christmas? By sinking the shafts of our spirits deep beneath the sparkling tinsel of the surface of Christmas and renewing within us the radiance of the inner meaning of the season. By rediscovering the faith and simplicity of a little child, for of such is the Kingdom of Heaven. By resolving to give ourselves away in love, joy and devotion. By using the light of Christmas to guide us through the coming year.

SACRAMENT MEETING

SUNDAY, DECEMBER 4, 1983

BISHOP.........BRUCE NIELSON
1ST COUN.......ROBERT LAW
2ND COUN.......HAROLD STANGELAND

PRESIDING............Bishop Bruce Nielson
CONDUCTING...........Brother Bob Law
ORGANIST.............Sister Clara Purves
CHORISTER............Sister S. Burtenshaw

WELCOME AND ANNOUNCEMENTS: Brother Law

OPENING HYMN: #33 Far, Far Away on Judea's
              Plains

INVOCATION: By Invitation

WARD BUSINESS: Brother Law

SACRAMENT HYMN: # 178 God Loved Us,
                 So He Sent His Son

BLESSING AND PASSING OF THE SACRAMENT

TIME SET ASIDE FOR THE BEARING OF TESTIMONIES

CLOSING HYMN: # 219 I Heard the Bells on
               Christmas Day

BENEDICTION: By Invitation

*   *   *   *   *

DISMISS TO SUNDAY SCHOOL & PRIMARY

****

Interviews with the Bishop can be booked
through Brother Kent Gibb at 436-3874.

Announcements for the bulletin can be phone
to Diane Powelson at 436-0980 by Wednesday 9

ANNOUNCEMENTS

All families, couples, and single adults
are encouraged to obtain a new Family Home
Evening Resource Book. Contact Corey Wight
this Sunday or by phoning 433-5422.
Cost is $3.00

Remember to mark your calendars for the
Ward Christmas Party on December 16th.
A turkey supper is planned. Sign-up lists
for salads and desserts are available in
Relief Society.
Children's Christmas Party will be on
December 23rd. More information will be
announced later.

Sister Nola Jackson has lost her looseleaf
notebook with her personal history and
goals, plans for coming year. It was
left under the Choir seats last Sunday.
If anyone has picked it up by mistake, or
knows of its whereabouts, PLEASE call her
or talk with her today. She is VERY anxious
to have it returned.

Tithing Settlement will start when the
financial records arrive from Salt Lake.

        What can I give Him
     Poor as I am ?
        If I were a shepherd
     I would give Him a lamb,
        If I were a Wise Man,
     I would do my part, -
        But what can I give Him,
     Give Him my heart.

                    - Christina G. Rossetti

By MARJORIE HOLMES

Thoughts on the true meaning of generosity

Priceless Gift

Give me true generosity at Christmas, Lord. A generosity that doesn't get confused with pride or extravagance. May our family's cards, our tree, our parties, our decorations be all in the spirit of loving celebration of a glorious event—and not in the desire to impress.

Let me give with the zeal of my own children who will labor half the night to make something or spend every long-saved or hard-earned penny to buy something for somebody they love—not to show off, but because it is a glorious thing to give ungrudgingly even at personal sacrifice.

Help me, above all, to remember that the family we honor and worship at Christmas was poor, very poor. They couldn't afford a fine hotel even if there had been room. They were happy to take shelter in a humble stable. They did not demand the best crib, the latest toys or the finest garments for the child you sent. They were grateful to wrap him in swaddling clothes and place him in a manger.

God, fill me, too, with that same shining sense of gratitude so that it is not the price-tag-ridden emotions that dominate at Christmas, but joy in your priceless gift.

Grant me true generosity at Christmas, Lord. A generosity of spirit that is rooted in thankfulness.

In his song "Stout-Hearted Men" Oscar Hammerstein said, "A heart can inspire other hearts with its fire." Then he said,

> Give me some men who are stout-hearted men,
> Who will fight for the right they adore.
> Start me with ten who are stout-hearted men,
> And I'll soon give you ten thousand more.

We catch the spirit of Christmas and the spirit of righteousness from each other, and then we pass them around among our friends and neighbors. But the situation that causes these good gifts to be most highly contagious is when we are united in a sanctified home before a blazing yule log.

The songs we sing seem to be a little more meaningful and happy when they are sung around a glowing, friendly fire. Friendships also seem a little sweeter, family ties are made a little stronger, religion itself seems more holy and the home is more hallowed in the light of the Christmas fire. The fire of the yule log is supposed to burn out old hurts and destroy past wrongs in preparing the way for the bright new year that is to follow. And as the burning yule log releases the light and warmth from the sun into our homes, so the Spirit of him who was born in the Bethlehem manger releases God's many blessings into our lives.

The Christmas fire might also serve us as a stimulating symbol for our eternal lives. The destiny of those who follow Christ is to become like him. If you would like your Christmas imagination stirred to its height, read the description of the resurrected Jesus given by John the Revelator while he was serving out his exile on the lonely Isle of Patmos. John said that he was in the spirit on the Lord's day when he heard a great voice behind him, as of the voice of a trumpet. He turned to see who had spoken to him, and he said he saw "one like unto the Son of man." Then, in trying to picture this magnificent being who stood before him, John said that he was "clothed with a garment down to the foot, and girt about . . . with a golden girdle. His head and his hairs were white like wool, as white as snow; and his eyes were as a flame of fire." (Revelation 1:13-14.)

We are familiar with the twinkle that great happiness sometimes puts in people's eyes. We sometimes describe this particular quality by saying, "He has a light in his eye," or "His face beams," or "His countenance shines." Then suppose we try to understand the celestial accomplishment that John attempted to describe when he said, "His eyes were as a *flame* of fire." The twinkle had now been magnified a million times. Elsewhere the scripture informs us that God is such a glorious personage that mortal man in his natural state would wither and die in his presence. Then contemplate our own situation when the impurities have all been eliminated from our lives by the atonement of Christ so that we may be admitted to that celestial order of which God himself is a member. How appropriate at Christmastime to light the yule log as we commemorate the birth of him from whom all blessings come.

As we worship our Heavenly Father and as we light the fires of faith and righteousness in our own lives, we may hear a little more clearly the song of the angels as well as God's own promise of our redemption. This will help us carry the spirit of *his* life from Christmas throughout the year.

The Christmas Angels

IF SOMEONE WERE to ask us to identify the most important event
that ever took place upon this earth, what would it be? Some
might mention various things such as the development of medi-
cal science, the invention of the printing press, or the discovery
of atomic power. For the most important event some people
would center their minds on the Christmas season and the all-
important fact that more than nineteen hundred years ago, the
Son of God was born in a manger in Bethlehem of Judea. There
are many reasons why this might easily qualify as the greatest
event that our earth has known.

He came here as the Savior of the world and the Redeemer
of all of the people who ever had or who ever would live upon
it. He came here by the direct appointment of God, his Father.
Under the authority of his appointment he established the
Church to give all of the people of the world an opportunity to
belong to it. He staffed his church with divinely appointed men
and taught those doctrines which, if believed in and followed,
would bring about the eternal exaltation of all mankind.

What other possible event could ever compare with this?
To begin with, any birth is one of the great miracles that no one
understands very much about. There are some people who
claim that they cannot believe in the literal bodily resurrection
nor in the everlasting continuance of the human soul. It has always seemed to me that this should never be very difficult for
anyone who can believe in his own birth. That is, if you can believe that two microscopic bits of protoplasm can come together
to create a life cell, and then by a process of self-division created
other cells completely unlike the original to make this great masterpiece of flesh and blood and bone and tissue and personality
and vision that we call a human being—if you can believe in that,
it ought not to be very difficult to believe that after that great
creation had once been established, it could continue on indefi-
nitely.

Edwin Markham once put this idea into verse under the title "The Unbelievable." He said:

Impossible, you say, that man survives the grave?
That there are other lives?
More strange, O friend, that we should ever rise
From out the dark to walk beneath the skies,
But having risen to life and light,
We need not wonder at our deathless flight,
Life is the unbelievable,
But now that this incredible has taught us how,
We can believe the all-imagining power
That breathed the cosma forth as golden flower
Had potence in his breath,
And plans us new surprises beyond death—
New spaces and new goals for the adventure of ascending souls,
Be brave, O heart, be brave,
It is not strange that man survives the grave.
T'would be a stranger thing were he destroyed,
Than that he ever vaulted from the void.

And thoughtful people never cease to wonder at this tremendous miracle that from this simple union of cells could come such master creations as George Washington, Abraham Lincoln, Winston Churchill, Moses, Enoch, Abraham, and the apostle Paul. And from such an unpromising beginning may come the master minds of science, industry, and invention. But by long odds, the greatest man who ever lived was known to us as Jesus of Nazareth. However, he was also known by name, character, and his good works long before Bethlehem. Actually he was ordained to his divine earthly destiny long before this earth was ever formed. All of the prophets from Adam down have known of his coming. The announcement of his birth in Bethlehem was made by an angel of great authority and power who had come from the presence of God. This personal messenger from the courts of heaven introduced himself by saying:

"I am Gabriel, that stand in the presence of God; and am sent to speak unto thee, and to shew thee these glad tidings." (Luke 1:19.)

Then he was sent to a young woman named Mary, who lived in Nazareth of Galilee, and he said to her: "The Holy Ghost shall come upon thee, and the power of the Highest shall overshadow thee: therefore also that holy thing which shall be born of thee shall be called the Son of God." (Luke 1:35.)

Luke also tells of the angel's announcement to the shepherds. He said: "And there were in the same country shepherds abiding in the field, keeping watch over their flock by night.

"And, lo, the angel of the Lord came upon them, and the glory of the Lord shone round about them: and they were sore afraid.

"And the angel said unto them, Fear not: for, behold, I bring you good tidings of great joy, which shall be to all people." (Luke 2:8-10.)

"And suddenly there was with the angel a multitude of the heavenly host praising God, and saying,

"Glory to God in the highest, and on earth peace, good will toward men." (Luke 2:13-14.)

It is a very interesting fact that Jesus Christ is a person. Before his birth he was a personage of spirit. During his mortality he was a personage of spirit that had been added upon with a destructible body of flesh and bones. After the resurrection he was a person with an indestructible body inseparably joined together with his immortal spirit. God the Father is also a person.

It is also a very interesting fact that God, angels, spirits, and men are all of the same species in different stages of development and in different degrees of righteousness. It is also very important that we understand that angels are also people. In addition, they are very important people. They are all a part of the family of God. We have the sure word of the Lord that all of those people who have or who will minister to the inhabitants of this earth are those who have been connected with it in the past or who will be connected with it in the future. (See D&C 130:5.)

One translation of the scriptures says of man that he was made "for a little while lower than the angels." Inasmuch as we are so closely connected with the angels, we ought to know as much as possible about them. The scriptures mention many angels by name. It has been revealed that Michael the Archangel (or head angel) came here to the earth as Adam, the great progenitor of the race. It has also been made known to us that Gabriel, who made the announcement, was Noah, that great prophet who the scripture says walked with God.

Of course, before the resurrection was initiated upon this earth by Jesus, those who were sent here as messengers were either in the unembodied or disembodied state. But in that great plan that God made for our evolution and growth, all of the righteous spirits, including the Son of God himself, were permitted to come here to the earth and obtain for themselves one of these wonderful, beautiful bodies of flesh and bones, without which no one could ever receive a fulness of joy, either here or hereafter.

Because Satan and his followers rebelled against God and were cast out, a mortal body and other privileges of mortality were denied them. Therefore, all of their progression was stopped. The mortal embodiment of Jesus adds greatly to the spirit of Christmas. For what a tremendous occasion it must have been when the time came for the First Begotten Son of God in the spirit to be begotten by God in the flesh and receive his body and the other wonderful blessings of mortality.

He also redeemed us from death, initiated the universal resurrection for all of earth's children, and made it possible for all of the spirit children of God to have a glorious eternal life on condition of our repentance and obedience to him. It is no wonder that such an occasion should be met with the greatest interest both on the earth and in heaven. Even the great Gabriel himself could not have been resurrected and gone on to perfection if the Son of God, a member of the first presidency of heaven, had not broken the bonds of death and made the resurrection possible. And, of course, before Jesus could do this, he had to be born and gain his own power over death.

No wonder this great multitude of the heavenly host came here for this occasion praising God and singing anthems of eternal worship and gratitude to him. Not only were the angels real people, but they had a very personal interest in what was going on.

Recently an article appeared in the press which said that of all of the scientists who have ever lived upon the earth, eighty percent of them are alive now. And certainly a very large percentage of those who stood among the noble and great in the council of God may also be alive now as we live in the greatest of all dispensations.

The apostle Paul looked forward to our time and referred to it as the dispensation of the fulness of times. It is referred to as the time of restitution of all things when all things will be brought together as one. And as God and men are both an important part of Christmas, so are the Christmas angels.

Since the creation of Adam, a great many angels have been sent from God's presence to our planet with various messages for our benefit. On one occasion an angel asked Adam why he offered sacrifice, and he said, "I know not, save the Lord commanded me." (Moses 5:6.) Frequently angels have been mistaken for mortal men. They are all a part of the same family. Even Jesus, the very Son of God himself, was not especially distinguished from others, and men said, "Is not this Joseph the carpenter's son?" The apostle Paul says that we should be careful how we entertain strangers because some have entertained angels unawares.

But just a few years ago all of us lived with God and all of us may have been angels. Certainly we served him in some capacity, Angels were sent to destroy the ancient cities of Sodom and Gomorrah. Angels ministered to Jesus in Gethsemane and while he was upon the cross. While he was being arrested, he affirmed the solemn fact that he could command the services of twelve legions of angels to fight in his behalf. Angels are very intelligent people. In heaven our brothers and sisters walk by sight, whereas we are now trying to learn to walk a little way by faith. Those of us who live upon the earth are just now beginning to learn a few things about space travel used so effectively by the Christmas angels nearly twenty centuries ago. Those living in heaven know a great many other things presently unknown to us.

When a university inaugurates a new president, the custom is for many other universities to send delegates to the inauguration. Everyone in heaven and upon the earth had a personal and vital interest in the birth of their Savior, and among that vast delegation that visited in Bethlehem there must have been representatives from all dispensations and all peoples. And some of us were undoubtedly among that angelic company. We remember that Moses and Elijah came as angels and ministered to Jesus on the high mountain when he was transfigured and appeared before Peter, James, and John in shining garments.

After the resurrection of Jesus, Matthew says: "And the graves were opened; and many bodies of the saints which slept arose, And came out of the graves after his resurrection, and went into the holy city, and appeared unto many." (Matthew 27: 52-53.) And since that time, many other people have become resurrected beings.

Through Malachi, God said: "Behold, I will send you Elijah the prophet before the coming of the great and dreadful day of the Lord: And he shall turn the heart of the fathers to the children, and the heart of the children to their fathers, lest I come and smite the earth with a curse." (Malachi 4:5-6.) Elijah not only ministered to Jesus on the Mount of Transfiguration over 800 years after he was taken into heaven, but he also appeared, some 2,600 years after being taken into heaven, to the Prophet Joseph Smith and Oliver Cowdery in the Kirtland Temple on April 3, 1836, in fulfillment of the word of the Lord through Malachi.

In his vision into the future from his lonely Isle of Patmos exile, John the Revelator said: "And I saw another angel fly in the midst of heaven, having the everlasting gospel to preach unto them that dwell on the earth, and to every nation, and kindred, and tongue, and people, Saying with a loud voice, Fear God, and give glory to him; for the hour of his judgment is come. . . ." (Revelation 14:6-7.)

In response to this revelation, the angel Moroni came and restored the gospel. Other angels have come in our day to restore many keys, authorities, and information that have been taken away from the earth because of apostasy.

The Christmas angels came to celebrate Christ's birth and implement his work upon the earth. But his first coming foreshadows and is closely related to his yet-future glorious second coming. And as we commemorate the birth of the Son of God and pay honor to the wise men and the shepherds, we ought not to forget that great group of angels or servants or messengers who had such a prominent part in Christmas and have been so helpful at other times in carrying forward the work of the Lord. We will also have many additional contacts with them in the future, including the occasion when Christ shall come again. May God help us to do our part with equal excellence.

The Gifts of Christmas

WE HAVE AN interesting custom among us wherein we set aside special days on which we think about special things. We set aside the second Sunday in May as Mother's Day, and on this day we let our minds reach up and try to understand the purposes for which this day was set apart. We set aside the third Sunday in June as Father's Day for the same purpose. And someone has said that the human mind has some of the qualities of the tendrils of a climbing vine. It tends to attach itself and draw itself upward by what it is put in contact with.

Then we have some other wonderful days in which we put our minds in contact with other great ideas. We have Memorial Day and Easter and Labor Day and the Fourth of July. We set aside the fourth Thursday in November as Thanksgiving, and on that day we try to build up our gratitude and appreciation, and as we recount our blessings we increase them. We set aside one day for Flag Day and one day for Washington's Birthday and one day for Citizenship Day. But we set aside an entire season for Christmas. The Christmas period generally begins before Thanksgiving and runs until after the New Year. The reason for this great difference in emphasis is that Christmas is probably the most important event in the year. Christmas also represents our greatest ideals and the most profitable ideals of our lives.

Someone has pointed out that a thing is not only important for itself alone, but it is often even more important for what it is a sign of, and what it stands for, what it gets us to think about, and what it impels us to do. Once each week we celebrate one day as the Sabbath day. That is a day set apart as a day of rest, a day of worship, and a day of rejoicing. Christmas is a kind of Sabbath for the entire year. Christmas is a season for worship and adoration. It is also commemorated as the birthday of the Savior of the world. The most important day in the life of every human being is the day on which He was born. That is the time when we were granted that greatest of all of our gifts, which is life.

Henry Thoreau, an early American philosopher, once said that we should thank God every day of our lives for the privilege of having been born, and then he went on to speculate on the rather unique supposition of what it might have been like if we had never been born, and he pointed out some of the many benefits that we would have missed as a consequence. Try to imagine what it would have been like if you had never been born or if your parents had never been born.

But what Mr. Thoreau may not have known was that one-third of all of the children of God never were born, and never can be born because they failed to pass the requirements of their first estate. This great group of God's spirit children followed Lucifer in his rebellion against God, with the result that the advantages of mortality were denied forever to them. If we fully understood, nothing could be more thrilling than a realization of the great blessings earned during our first estate.

And nothing could be more plainly written in the scriptures than the fact that the life of Christ did not begin at Bethlehem; neither did it end on Calvary. Jesus said, "I came forth from the Father and am come into the world." Again, "I leave the world and go unto the Father."

It is just as plainly written in the scriptures that our lives did not begin when we were born, neither will they end when we die. We are all the children of God, endowed with his attributes and made heirs to his glory. The purposes of his birth were many. He came that we might have life and have it more abundantly. He came to establish his church, to teach us proper conduct, to make us aware of the doctrines of truth, to redeem us from death, and to help us bring about our own eternal glory and everlasting happiness.

Actually, December 25 is not the real anniversary of his birth. He was born in the spring while the shepherds were watching their flocks upon the hills of Judea. In a modern revelation, the Lord has made known that the actual anniversary of his birth was the sixth day of April. (D&C 20:1 and 21:3.) And he reestablished his church upon the earth in our day on the 1830th anniversary of his birth in Bethlehem. However, the day on which we commemorate his birth may not be nearly as important as how we commemorate it. Because his birth is so important, we actually should commemorate it every day in the year. His birth is highly significant to us for many reasons. We think about the many joys of Christmas, the convictions of Christmas, and the miracles of Christmas, but among our greatest blessings are the gifts of Christmas.

God is the giver of all good gifts. And God sent his only Begotten Son into the world to redeem us from death. It is his gift to us that whosoever believeth in him and obeys his laws should not perish but have everlasting life. Then to symbolize this spirit of giving, the wise men from the East traveled across the desert and laid their own gifts of gold, frankincense, and myrrh at the feet of their newborn king. We have continued this interesting custom of giving, and as an important part of the festivities of this holy day, we give presents to each other. Actually, that is one of our finest ideas.

A few years ago I heard an important businessman say that all of us have a natural obligation to give something to everyone we meet every time that we meet him. I thought of this idea the other day as I met a good friend of mine while I was walking down the street. I was very pleased to see him, as every meeting with him is always pleasant, and I shook his hand and put my arm around him as we joked and laughed and visited. He is not only a friendly, pleasant, and happy person, but he is also very thoughtful, constructive, and inspirational. Our short interchange probably lasted only for about two minutes, but as I went on my way down the street, I was aware of how much better I felt. My step was more easy, my enthusiasm was greater, the day seemed a little brighter, and everything seemed to me to be so much more worthwhile. I now felt as though I were about ten feet tall. Not only was my interest in life greater, but I also felt that my life expectancy had been increased. I was not only grateful for him, but I was also grateful for what I was while I was with him.

John D. Rockefeller had an interesting and tangible way of carrying out the symbolism of this idea of giving everyone something. He was the world's first billionaire, and everyone thought of him in terms of his financial success. Therefore, he used to begin each day with a pocket full of shiny new silver dimes. Then to everyone he met, he gave one of his shiny new ten-cent silver coins.

On one occasion an important man asked Peter and John for alms. Peter said: "Silver and gold have I none; but such as I have give I thee: In the name of Jesus Christ of Nazareth rise up and walk." (Acts 3:6.)

We all give "such as we have." John D. Rockefeller gave dimes. That is wonderful, and I would like to have had one of Mr. Rockefeller's dimes. But think what a great teacher or a loving parent or a devoted friend can give. How many millions of dimes would it take to equal the value of the great idea that we can all give. Every time Mr. Rockefeller gave a dime his store was diminished, but every time we give faith, encouragement, and a love of the truth, our own supply is increased. We can make each other rich by setting a good example and manifesting a real love for and confidence in each other.

Someone once said that he could never figure out what to give for Christmas as everyone already had everything. The next day in the mail he received a suggested list which said: "Give to your enemy forgiveness, to your opponent tolerance, to your friend your heart, to a customer service, to all men charity, to every child a good example, and to yourself respect." Most of us need lots of gifts, as we are all near paupers in those greatest gifts which cost us nothing. We can even give to ourselves those great gifts of character, personality, religion, faith, good attitudes, and a grateful, happy heart. And there are some things that we can give to others that even God himself cannot. That is, there is no particular point in asking God to forgive our enemies, because that is something that only we ourselves can do. And what about a prayer in which we say to God, "Make me gentle, industrious, honest, religious, considerate, and fair." That is a prayer that even he cannot answer without our help.

When we pray "Forgive us our debts, as we forgive our debtors," we are agreeing that the quality of our answers will depend entirely upon us. This is also related to the petition in which we say, "Give us this day our daily bread." It has been said that 95 percent of all the ingredients that go into making a crop of wheat have already been provided by the Creator. That is, he has already prepared the topsoil, the air, the water, the climate, and the sunshine with which a bumper crop may be produced. All we need to do is to furnish the other 5 percent. We can also fulfill the divine promise saying, ". . . before they call, I will answer; and while they are yet speaking, I will hear." (Isaiah 65:24.)

What a tremendous gift we are given with the authority and power to answer so many of our own prayers. The Lord has said: "There is a law, irrevocably decreed in heaven before the foundations of this world, upon which all blessings are predicated —And when we obtain any blessing from God, it is by obedience to that law upon which it is predicated." (D&C 130:20-21.) Usually God has already done his part even before our prayer is uttered. But we fail God and we fail ourselves when we ask Deity to do everything while we do nothing but pray. We remember what someone has said, that "the hands that help are holier than the lips that pray."

I have a book at my desk entitled *The Great Sermons of the World*. It was compiled by Clarence E. McCartney. It contains what, in Mr. McCartney's opinion, are the greatest sermons ever given in our world. A couple of these sermons were delivered by a preacher by the name of Whitefield, who lived up in New England a couple of hundred years ago. By way of apology, Mr. McCartney said that no one could listen to the sermons of Whitefield and understand why it was that thousands of people were always flocking out to hear him. And then by way of explanation, he said that you can't get the man on the paper. You can get his words and his questions and his ideas, but you can't get the man. You can't get the light in his eye or the music of his voice or the contagion of his spirit on the paper. You can't capture on the paper the fire of his enthusiasm or the sweep of his personality or the radio activity of his soul.

Someone has said that there are no real gifts except when we give of ourselves. All gifts of wealth or jewels are just imitations or substitutions of the real thing. John D. Rockefeller's dimes were just a part of the result of his success. The real success was in Mr. Rockefeller. We can only give ourselves to each other when we keep ourselves givable. A husband bound down in sin can't give himself to his wife because he doesn't have himself to give. A wife who has been enslaved by hate cannot give herself to her husband. Neither can we give righteousness and peace to our children when we don't have them to give.

The greatest gifts have been given to us by Deity. We have been given life. We have been given our free agency. He has given us the ability for an unlimited industry. The Savior of the world has established his church upon the earth and has revealed the truths of eternal life. He has given us the earth itself. He has given us his Spirit. He has given us the greatest opportunities and the finest principles of eternal life to live by.

In the will of Patrick Henry, he wrote as follows: "I have now disposed of all of my property to my family. There is one more thing I wish I could give them, and that is the Christian religion. If they had that and I had not given them one shilling, they would have been rich, and if they did not have that, though I have given them all the world, they would be poor."

As we think about the real gifts of Christmas, we should prepare our lives to receive them. For the greatest gifts have little value if we are not capable of receiving them. Christ was prevented from being born in the inn because all of the space had already been taken up. We must not keep our lives so full of sins and worldly thoughts that there will be no room for the joys and the gifts of Christmas. The greatest idea of our modern world is that God lives and that he desires us to have his most valuable gifts of Christmas.

The Glory of Christmas

EACH YEAR AS we commemorate Christmas, we are conscious of a spirit that distinguishes this season from all others. This difference might best be described as "The Glory of Christmas." We catch something of this spirit when we read those scriptural verses written by Luke in which the birth of Christ is announced to the world. What a great experience it must have been in that long ago Christmas night for the shepherds to see and hear an angel from the presence of God! The messenger came in great glory, authority, and power to deliver his message. But God's glory also enveloped the shepherds who received the message.

Some form of this term "glory" appears in the scriptures over 400 times. It is used to describe that quality of radiance and magnificence in the personality of God, as well as to picture God's dwelling place. Glory is one of the qualities that distinguishes the entire idea of Christmas, and when we get it into our hearts, it lifts us above the ordinary events of the rest of the year.

The dictionary says that glory is a resplendent beauty, or magnificence. It is a state of splendor, or absolute happiness. Glory also means exalted praise, honor, or distinction. It is something that makes a person illustrious. The scripture speaks of some people being "glorified." This is an act or process of exaltation. God is the most exalted of all beings, and therefore the most glorious. God is such a glorious personage that no one can endure his presence unless quickened by his Spirit.

We remember that after Moses had visited with God upon Mount Sinai, the glory of God rested upon Moses with such intensity that the children of Israel could not endure his presence, and therefore a covering had to be placed over his face to make it possible for them to communicate with him. In the Garden of Gethsemane on the last Thursday of his life, Jesus said to his Father, "I have glorified thee on the earth: I have finished the work which thou gavest me to do. And now, O Father,

glorify thou me with thine own self with the glory which I had
with thee before the world was." (John 17:4-5.)

On the following Sunday morning as he came forth in the
resurrection, a part of this prayer had already been answered,
and in his *immortal* presence the soldiers whom Pilate had
placed on guard to maintain the security of the tomb became as
dead men. These were not timid, easily frightened men; these
were hard, bold, courageous, seasoned soldiers of Rome who had
learned to stand in the presence of death without a quiver of
emotion. But now that they stood in the presence of a resurrected glorified life, they became as dead men.

The purpose of Christ's mission to the earth was to redeem
and glorify all of us. If we live as we should, it is reasonable to
expect that the offspring of God might eventually hope to become like the eternal parent, and we need to get started on this
important process as soon as possible. In speaking about this
to the Thessalonians, the apostle Paul says, "But we are bound
to give thanks alway to God for you, brethren beloved of the
Lord, because God hath from the beginning chosen you to salvation through sanctification of the Spirit and belief of the truth:
Whereunto he called you by our gospel, to the obtaining of the
glory of our Lord, Jesus Christ." (2 Thessalonians 2:13-14.) We
need not wait until eternity begins to start acquiring this quality.
Christmas is to help us get some of this glory into our lives now.

When I was in my earliest school years, a part of the first
day after the Christmas holidays was used in having each student stand up and tell the other members of the class what he
had received for Christmas. For the children from well-to-do
homes this seemed a pleasant experience, but the members of
poorer families were sometimes a little embarrassed because they
didn't always have as much to talk about. Sometimes when a
large family lives under difficult financial conditions, there aren't
always enough presents to go around.

But even as adults we still have the same question asked
and answered many times at Christmas. Someone is sure to ask
"What did you get for Christmas," and we may still feel a little
bit bad if we don't have an acceptable answer at least to ourselves. Everyone enjoys getting nice presents, and of course
Christmas means so many different things to so many different

people, and actually there are many kinds of Christmases. There is the child's Christmas—its symbol is the toy, and its chief characteristic is excitement. Then there is the world's Christmas. Its symbol is the Christmas tree, and its chief characteristic is festivity. Then there is the Christian's Christmas. Its symbol is the star, and its chief characteristic is the kind of righteousness that leads to the glory of God.

While God's glory surrounded the shepherds, the angels sang their Christmas anthems, saying, "Glory to God in the highest, and on earth peace, good will to men." When this glory is lacking in the world, then to that extent unrighteousness and unhappiness prevail. Christmas can be and sometimes is a very lonely time for some people under some circumstances. Some people might answer this question of "What did you get for Christmas?" by listing a sour stomach, a drunken headache, a mental depression, and the consciousness of a few extra steps taken along that broad road that leads to death. Those who celebrate Christmas the wrong way might feel a little bit embarrassed if they were asked to stand up and report before the class. And while we generally think of Christmas as a happy time, yet it is not always so. It can be a very serious tragedy when no one remembers us with a Christmas present, or a letter of love, or an expression of good will. It can also be tragic to have a memory of a Christmas without any glory in it.

We try to get glory into our lives at Christmastime by lighting up our cities, our homes, and our Christmas trees. This might in some way represent the glory that lighted up the Judean hills and the manger in Bethlehem on that long ago Christmas night. But there are other Christmas lights that shine out through people's faces, or well up out of their hearts. It would be difficult to think of God, or Gabriel, or others from God's presence without their glory, but *we* are God's children and we have been so created that glory may also be made to shine in us.

Archibald Rutledge once wrote a delightful little book entitled *My Colonel and His Lady.* In his book he tells of an interesting experience that he had as a lad on the Santee River in central South Carolina. This particular occasion has to do with an old Negro riverboat captain who piloted the ferryboat *Foam.* The boat was dirty, odorous, and badly kept. But one day when

Dr. Rutledge went down to the river, he found the *Foam* completely transformed. It was clean from stem to stern. It fairly glistened and gleamed in the sunlight. The boat's brass had been polished until it shone like so many mirrors. The bilge water had disappeared from behind the seats, and the deck had been scoured to the raw wood. No less miraculous was the transformation in the Negro captain himself. He was shining and immaculate. His face beamed, his eyes sparkled, as he sat behind the *Foam's* wheel with an open Bible on his lap.

When Dr. Rutledge asked the riverboat captain the reason for this wonderful transformation, he said, "I got a glory." That is, some great ideas had gotten into the captain's thinking and some great aspirations had gotten into his bloodstream. These had made him a different man. He now had the glory of a lighted mind, and the glory of a quickened personality. He also had the glory of a righteous ambition. Religion had touched him effectively in exactly the right places. But the transformation that was so apparent in the riverboat was only a manifestation of a more important transformation in the captain. The nature of his work itself had not changed; he was still a riverboat captain. But he was now the best riverboat captain on the Santee. Henceforth whatever he did would indicate his own change of life, and his life's work would indicate his life's glory.

The story of the riverboat captain is the story of everyone who gets a glory into his life. And what a great Christmas this would be if we all cleaned up our riverboats and got the glory of Christmas into our hearts. Like so many other things, a glory comes because of what we do. If one isn't glorious in what he does, then he isn't glorious. We can't get a glory in our hearts while the bilge water is still under our seats and in our attitudes. We can't have a glory and a chronic case of unrighteousness at the same time.

We have several descriptions of the physical glory of immortal beings. John gives us one in his book of Revelation. While on the Isle of Patmos some sixty years after the Savior's crucifixion on Calvary, John says that he was in the spirit on the Lord's day when he heard a great voice behind him as of the voice of a trumpet saying, "I am Alpha and Omega, the first and the last." John turned to see who had spoken to him, and he said he saw "one like unto the Son of man, clothed with a garment down to the foot, and girt about . . . with a golden girdle." He said that "his head and his hairs were white like wool, as white as snow; and his eyes were as a flame of fire; And his feet like unto fine brass, as if they were burned in a furnace; and his voice as the sound of many waters. . . . and his countenance was as the sun shineth in his strength." (Revelation 1:11-16.)

We often describe a quality in people by saying they have a light in their eyes or their faces beam or their countenances glow. But here these qualities might be magnified a few million times where John could say, "His eyes were as a flame of fire." The visits of heavenly messengers are not limited to Bethlehem and Patmos.

In the early spring of 1820 in upper New York State, the Father and the Son appeared to the Prophet Joseph Smith, who describes the experience as follows: ". . . I saw a pillar of light exactly over my head, above the brightness of the sun, which descended gradually until it fell upon me. . . . When the light rested upon me I saw two Personages, whose brightness and glory defy all description, standing above me in the air. One of them spake unto me, calling me by name and said, pointing to the other—*This is My Beloved Son. Hear Him!*" (Joseph Smith 2:16-27.)

Other heavenly messengers have also appeared upon the earth in our day. Joseph Smith describes a visit that he had with the angel Moroni on September 21, 1823, as follows: "While I was thus in the act of calling upon God, I discovered a light appearing in my room, which continued to increase until the room was lighter than at noonday, when immediately a personage appeared at my bedside, standing in the air, for his feet did not touch the floor.

"He had on a loose robe of most exquisite whiteness. It was a whiteness beyond anything earthly I had ever seen; nor do I believe that any earthly thing could be made to appear so exceedingly white and brilliant. His hands were naked, and his arms also, a little above the wrist; so, also, were his feet naked, as were his legs, a little above the ankles. His head and neck were also bare. I could discover that he had no other clothing on but this robe, as it was open, so that I could see into his bosom.

"Not only was his robe exceedingly white, but his whole person was glorious beyond description, and his countenance truly like lightning. The room was exceedingly light, but not so very bright as immediately around his person. When I first looked upon him, I was afraid; but the fear soon left me.

"He called me by name, and said unto me that he was a messenger sent from the presence of God to me, and his name was Moroni. . . ." (Joseph Smith 2:30-33.)

If God and angels had only been seen once, that would be proof that they still exist. One of the greatest glories of Christmas is the knowledge that God lives and that Jesus Christ is the Son of God who came to earth to help us get his glory into our lives. Our greatest Christmas ambition should be that we might be successful in making our own lives glorious.

The Christmas Tree

THE BIBLE GIVES us an interesting account of that great period in which God created the heavens and the earth and all that in them are. It would be very interesting to have a list of all the thousands of things that God created, such as the animals, birds, insects, and flowers, and try to know what the reasons were that prompted him to create them in the form he did, and what the purposes and destinies of their lives are. As one of the important parts of creation, the record says, "And I, the Lord God, planted a garden eastward in Eden, and there I put the man whom I had created. And out of the ground made I, the Lord God, to grow every tree, naturally, that is pleasant to the sight of man . . . and man saw that it was good for food." (Moses 3:8-9.)

There were two particular trees with very unusual abilities that were planted in the center of the garden. One of these was the tree of life and the other was the tree of knowledge of good and evil. Both of these trees have had and will have an important effect upon our human lives. The record says that when our first parents ate the fruit from the tree of knowledge of good and evil, a change came over them where they could distinguish between good and evil. And commenting on this change God said, "Behold, the man is become as one of us to know good from evil. . . ." (Moses 4:28.)

Someday we are going to experience another miraculous change when we earn the right to eat the fruit from the tree of life. In the meantime, our trees bless us in many ways with the vitamins, flavors, and strengths that come from their fruits, the beauty and fragrances of their flowers, and in a hundred other ways. In a very real sense, trees have life the same as human beings do. They sometimes almost seem to have human powers. Trees were first created by God in heaven the same as we were, and they also have spirits. In the Bible account of creation we read:

"And every plant of the field before it was in the earth, and every herb of the field before it grew: for the Lord God had not caused it to rain upon the earth, and there was not a man to till the ground." (Genesis 2:5.)

In addition to the tree of life and the tree of knowledge of good and evil, think of all of the other wonderful trees that God created for our benefit. Some of these trees are shade trees; others produce foods and fibers. A very important group of trees were designed by the Creator to provide us with lumber for our houses, barns, and many other types of construction. We have many magnificent flowering trees that produce great masses of blossoms and fill the atmosphere with perfumes that give us a feeling of happiness and exhilaration. There is a holly tree that provides us with berries and wreaths to make our great occasions more memorable. We have the wonder of the giant redwoods, which are the largest of all of God's earthly creations.

Some trees serve us as symbols of faith and emblems of accomplishment. We are inspired by the great oak tree, which reflects in us attitudes of stability, solidarity, and strength. Some trees are useful to us both for their utility and their symbolism, such as the pine tree, the spruce, and the fir tree. These have the interesting characteristic of being evergreen. They serve us on the special occasion of Christmas when we celebrate the birth of the Son of God.

There are many legends about how we got the idea of having what we call the Christmas tree. By some this tree is called the holy tree. It is said that the Christmas tree produces the wood of peace. Because of the fact that it is always green, it has become a symbol of eternal life. All over the world this evergreen tree is associated with Christmas and is called by such names as the Christmas tree or the tree of Christ.

We have an interesting Christmas song that originated in Germany a long time ago. It is entitled "O Tannenbaum," or translated, it is "O Christmas Tree." The English version is as follows:

> O Christmas tree, O Christmas tree,
> O tree of green, unchanging,
> Your boughs, so green in summertime,
> Do brave the snow of wintertime,
> O Christmas tree, O Christmas tree,
> O tree of green, unchanging.

O Christmas tree, O Christmas tree,
You set my heart a singing.
Like little stars, your candles bright
Send to the world a wondrous light
O Christmas tree, O Christmas tree,
You set my heart a singing.

O Christmas tree, O Christmas tree,
You come from God, eternal.
A symbol of the Lord of love
Whom God to man sent from above.
O Christmas tree, O Christmas tree,
You come from God, eternal.

O Christmas tree, O Christmas tree,
You speak of God, unchanging.
You tell us all to faithful be,
And trust in God eternally.
O Christmas tree, O Christmas tree,
You speak of God, unchanging.

This great tree always points its green spires up toward heaven, and standing as it does as the symbol of everlasting life, it also becomes one of the loveliest symbols of the most worthwhile things. It is reported that Martin Luther started the custom of setting up Christmas trees in our homes as we commemorate the birth of Christ. And with this tree's beauty, its fragrance, and its symbolism, it naturally becomes the center of our Christmas worship and festivities.

It is related that one night during a Christmas season many years ago, Martin Luther was walking through the forest. He was thinking about Christmas. And his heart was also filled with the wonder and beauty of God's natural creations. As he looked up through the beautiful forest of evergreen trees toward the stars, the trees and the stars seemed to blend with and become a part of each other. And the loveliness of the evening made the scene particularly pleasant.

He was greatly motivated with the fragrance of the evergreen in his lungs, their beauty in his eyes, and their symbolism in his heart. The stars were so low and bright that they seemed like ornaments decorating the forest trees; and some of the great stars, standing above the treetops, were reminiscent of that famous star which led the wise men across the desert and stood above the stable at Bethlehem.

All of these forest trees seemed to be pointing Martin Luther up toward God. Then when the breezes blew through the needles they sounded as if God's angels were playing anthems of praise on heavenly instruments. Under these circumstances it was not difficult for him to go back in his mind and absorb the joy and worship of that first Christmas night long ago on the Judean hills.

Martin Luther wanted his family to enjoy this satisfying sight, and so he selected a particularly beautiful and shapely tree that seemed to have an appropriate personality and character. He cut it down and set it up in his home. Then he decorated it with lighted candles and tinsel and colored ornaments to make it shine out in all of its natural brightness and beauty. He was trying to represent to his family what he had seen and felt in the garden of God's great outdoor forest.

At Christmastime the Christmas tree always points us upward toward God; its evergreen qualities symbolize to us our own eternal life, and its stars and other ornaments fill our houses and our lives with beauty and a meaningful significance. In addition, there has always been an inspiring relationship between light and life. The scripture says of Jesus: "In him was life; and the life was the light of men." (John 1:4.) The scripture mentions the light of truth and it says:

"Which truth shineth. This is the light of Christ. As also he is in the sun, and the light of the sun, and the power thereof by which it was made.

"And the light which shineth, which giveth you light, is through him who enlighteneth your eyes, which is the same light that quickeneth your understandings;

"Which light proceedeth forth from the presence of God to fill the immensity of space—

"The light which is in all things, which giveth life to all things, which is the law by which all things are governed, even the power of God who sitteth upon his throne, who is in the bosom of eternity, who is in the midst of all things." (D&C 88:7, 11-13.)

We might try to understand what our situation would be like without this light of Christ. Before that early morning of creation, our earth was without form and void, and a brooding unbroken darkness covered the face of the deep. Then just try to imagine what it must have been like when in the march of progress God first said, "Let there be light." The same thing might well have been said when he was born into the world. Later in his ministry he himself said, "I am the light of the world: he that followeth me shall not walk in darkness, but shall have the light of life." (John 8:12.)

How appropriate that the Christmas tree, which is the symbol of everlasting life, should also be lighted with the most beautiful kinds and colors of lights. The Christmas tree is very closely associated with another Christmas tradition, which centers around the yule log. The tree from which the yule log is cut might have been growing in the forest for a hundred summers. During all of this long time it was gathering up and storing the sunshine, warmth, and energy that come from God's great central warehouse of the sun.

It is interesting for us to remember that as great as our earth is, yet it is not an independent earth. If the sun's rays were turned off for just a few hours, no life could exist here. At this very instant God is sending us billions of tons of food, vitamins, flavors, tastes, energy, health, and strength from the sun. They come to us through 93 million miles of cold dead space and are only released when they reach our atmosphere. The sun's rays also cure both mental and physical diseases and provide us with physical and moral strength.

This great tree that grows in the forest stores up within itself this warmth, life, and light for a hundred summers. And then the tree is ceremoniously cut to provide our Christmas fire. And as the log burns, it releases inside the home the warmth, sunshine, and gladness that it has stored away during all of these years so that even when it may be cold and unpleasant outside, our burning yule log brings inside our homes and gets into the lives of our family members all of those blessings which come from God that are captured by his invention of trees. In addition, what a great delight it is to surround the burning yule log at Christmastime as we commemorate the Savior's birth by singing Christmas carols and recounting the delightful traditions of Christmas. We also make expressions of love to each other; we give ourselves to each other when we give the gifts that have a little greater significance because they have been placed under the Christmas tree.

While the tree's natural fragrance fills the house with perfume, the crackling of the Christmas fire and the warmth that comes from our own hearts help us to fill our souls with that spirit of worship of him who is the author of our salvation, the finisher of our faith, and the Savior of our souls. In dens of sin it is customary to turn down the lights. But at Christmastime we are prompted to turn on more light, not only in our homes but in our lives as well. Then we are further lifted up as we spiritually adapt the symbolism of the evergreen, which points us up to eternal lives.

During his teaching ministry Jesus took the ordinary things of life, such as the lilies of the field, the farmer sowing his grain, the fisherman with his nets, and the husbandman dressing his vines, and fashioned them into great spiritual truths that greatly upgrade our spirituality and strengthen our faith. No one lives unto himself alone, and no one can enjoy the greatest satisfactions of his soul by himself. We need each other and all of God's other creations to make our lives complete and happy. And Christmas also teaches us to get greater stimulations from all of the symbolism of his handiwork.

And so at this high point of our year, we ornament our Christmas trees, burn our yule logs, turn on the lights that come from God to assist us to get back into his presence. We also stimulate ourselves to develop those great gifts of love and worship that he has implanted in our souls.

The High Places of Christmas

AMONG EARLY-DAY peoples, before the days of temples, it was customary to erect altars on hill tops. These special places of worship were called "high places." One of the most famous of these was located at Gibeon, where young King Solomon used to go to offer sacrifices and where the Lord appeared to him in a dream and said, "Ask what I shall give thee." (2 Chronicles 1:7.) God seems to have favored this custom of meeting with his servants in high places. He called Moses up to the top of Mount Sinai to spend those memorable forty days. It was from Mount Sinai that God gave the Ten Commandments. Moses spent his last mortal hours on the top of Mount Nebo. Jesus himself often went to the mountains.

It was on a high mountain where he was transfigured and appeared in shining garments with Moses and Elias before Peter, James, and John. The greatest of all human discourses was the Sermon on the Mount. And Jesus ascended to his Father in heaven from the top of Mount Olivet.

If I had the words and ability to make you feel the spirit of Christmas, I would take you to some of those high places of Christmas thought. The most important thing that anyone ever gets out of Christmas is the Christmas spirit. At its best, this is the spirit of worship, the spirit of service, the spirit of Christ.

But all of our Christmases, as well as our lives themselves, are lived on several different levels. There is a constant ebb and flow in our lives. We have some upbeats and some downbeats. There are some high tides and some low tides in all of the things that we do. Suppose we explore some of the various levels of Christmas.

Level No. 1 is the level of joy and gaiety. Christmas is the time of our greatest happiness. During this period we sing Christmas carols and listen to sacred Christmas anthems and inspiring oratorios. We have parties, feasting, and celebrations. And we increase the Christmas spirit as we develop our own happiness level.

Level No. 2 is the level of beauty and festivity. We decorate our cities, our streets, and the outside and inside of our homes. More than any other holiday, Christmas is home-centered.

Level No. 3 is that of our Christmas communication and giving. This custom was started by the wise men who followed the star across the desert and laid their presents at the feet of the newborn King. We also increase our visiting at Christmastime. In addition, we send our millions of beautiful, highly colored Christmas cards and we give many useful and beautiful presents. Sometimes we accuse ourselves of commercialism. Some business houses may do as much business during the Christmas season as they do in all of the rest of the year put together. But this has many good points. We sell more good books at Christmastime than at any other period. And no one would ever think of giving a shoddy or a dirty book for Christmas.

A large part of this greater business activity is because of our gifts of clothing, food, and beautiful things. Some philosopher once said that the only real gifts are those gifts that we make of ourselves. "All other gifts," said he, "are merely imitations of gifts." But the more we think about it, the more we are convinced that almost all gifts are gifts of ourselves.

Each one of us has been assigned to carry on some part of the work of the world, for which we usually receive some material compensation. Each day as we expend our energy and capability, we are exhausting some portion of our strength and the money that is given us in exchange for our life's energy. That is, our industry is being made negotiable and transferable.

It is pretty difficult to get along without money, and even though it may be called commercialism by some people, yet money represents our labor with which we buy books, presents, and Christmas cards. We can build temples and send out missionaries and provide college educations and buy flowers for our wives with that part of us that we have made negotiable through our work.

Level No. 4 of Christmas has to do with the great traditions and the great literature of Christmas. Each year we love to recount the thrilling story of the star that appeared in the East and led the wise men across the desert. We think about the shepherds who were watching their flocks by night upon the hills of Judea and to whom the announcement of the Savior's birth was made. And then we visualize that great concourse of angels who had come from the presence of God to welcome the newborn King of the earth, which he himself had created. We might also try to understand what kind of young woman Mary must have been to have been chosen to be the mother of the Son of God, the greatest being who ever lived upon our planet.

But all of us are wonderful people. Someone has said, "There are no ordinary people." The most ordinary kind of person with whom you ever have anything to do, if you could see the veils of his mortality drawn aside, may be the kind of person that you would feel like falling down and worshiping before. That is, if you could have seen Abraham as he tended his flocks on the plains of Palestine, you may have thought of him as a rather ordinary kind of shepherd. But if you could have seen Abraham as he stood among the noble and great in the council of God, or if you could look in on Abraham at this instant as he lives and rules with God, it may be that you would think of him on a little higher level of importance. The apostle Paul said that we should be careful how we entertain strangers because some have entertained angels unawares.

But who are we? One translation of the scripture says that we are made for a little while lower than the angels. But many of us were also once among the noble and great in the council of God. All of us were in his presence a hundred years ago and were then his angels. And when we get married, have children, and conduct our family home evenings, we are also entertaining angels.

On two of the levels of Christmas we are greatly inspired by the personal life of Christ. One is the inspiration we get from him as a man and the other is the inspiration we get from him as God. Even at age twelve he was teaching the wise men in the temple. Before his short three-year ministry had been concluded, he had earned the right to be called the Great Teacher, the Master, the Great Physician, the Worker of Miracles. J. A. Francis makes an appraisal of this most outstanding character by saying:

Here is a man who grew up in an obscure village, the child of a poor peasant woman. He worked in a carpenter shop until he was thirty, and then for three years he was an itinerant preacher.

He never wrote a book. He never held an office. He never owned a home. He never had a family. He never went to college. He never put his foot inside a big city. He never traveled two hundred miles from the place where he was born.

While still a young man, the tide of popular opinion turned against him. His friends ran away. One of them denied him. Another betrayed him. He went through the mockery of a trial. He was nailed upon the cross between two thieves. While he was dying his executioners gambled for the only thing he owned, which was his cloak. When he was dead, he was laid in a borrowed tomb through the pity of a friend.

But since then nineteen wide centuries have come and gone, and today he is the very center of the human race. I am well within the mark when I say that all of the armies that ever marched, and all of the navies that were built, and all of the parliaments that ever sat, and all of the kings that ever reigned, put together, have not affected the life of man upon this earth as powerfully as has this one solitary life.

Then we come to the highest level of Christmas—that of Christ as God. The biographies of most great men start out on the day that they were born. However, to adequately understand the life of Christ, we must go a long way back beyond that point. Nothing is more clearly written in the scripture than the fact that the life of Christ did not begin at Bethlehem. Neither did it end on Calvary. He said, "I came forth from the Father and am come into the world. Again I leave the world and go unto the Father." In his memorable prayer in the garden he said, "And now, O Father, glorify thou me with thine own self with the glory which I had with thee before the world was." (John 17:5.)

Our lives are so closely related to his that they can best be studied together. And it is just as plainly written in the scripture that none of our lives began at our birth and neither will they end when we die.

All of the prophets from the time of Adam knew a great deal about the life of Christ long before he was born. Jesus said to the Jews: "Before Abraham was, I am." He is called Emanuel, meaning "God with us." He is the King of kings, the Lord of lords. He gave his life to redeem us from death. He led the forces in the war in heaven to preserve our individual free agency, and we were associated with him and were under his direction through all of the interesting experiences of that first estate. We know a great deal about his life during that period. In writing the life of Christ, the scriptures also tell us a great deal about his third estate, and as we look back to Bethlehem and the Creation, so we also look forward to that wonderful period beyond the boundaries of mortality.

We know that Christ is scheduled very soon to come again to the earth. This time he will come in power and great glory, with all of his holy angels with him to execute judgment upon all the ungodly and to inaugurate upon our earth his millennial reign of a thousand years of peace and happiness, when the work of this world will be finished. This will be in preparation for this great winding-up scene of our earth's history and the final judgment. Then this earth will be dedicated as the celestial kingdom of God for those who have lived here upon it and who have qualified to live here eternally. We know about the glorious place that is contemplated for those who are faithful to God, and if we have conformed our lives to him, then we will have an eternal high place in God's presence forever.

Home for Christmas

AMONG THE IMPORTANT marvels of our lives are the beauty, utility, and comfort of this great earth fashioned as a place for us to live. And in a very profitable and interesting way, each of us has been given a kind of unlimited possession of it. Someone has said, "I own the landscape." And in some very real ways, each of us individually owns the great mountains, the beautiful forests, and the life-giving rivers. We feast on the earth's beauty to our heart's content and it provides us with some of the finest places for recreation and inspiration. As we cultivate our share of the earth's topsoil, it is made productive by the rainfall, the sunshine, the atmosphere, and the rotation of the earth. Then we exchange our products for those produced by people living in other areas of the earth. Our earth gives us almost unlimited privileges for sightseeing, which is our biggest business. We are also comparatively free to engage in fishing, hunting, education, and recreation almost on our own terms.

Everyone likes to go places and do things. We frequently go away to college. We often seek our fortunes in foreign lands. The highways are usually crowded and the airways are full of people who want to be some place other than where they are, and this is our privilege. But God has given us a more intense interest in some particular country and city. Someone has said: "God gave all men all earth to love, but since our hearts are small, ordained that just one place should be beloved over all." And we always like to come back home occasionally—at least for special events.

As the supreme focus of our world interest, God has ordained the home as a center around which our lives most happily and successfully revolve. Because the family is the greatest organization and Christmas is our most important event, they usually go best together. One of the chief characteristics of Christmas is that it is highly home-centered. And no matter where we may go during the year or what the purpose of our travels may be, everyone always wants to be home for Christmas. Then how tragic it is and how lonesome it can become when we have no home to go to.

Recently I talked with a fine mother whose husband and children had been unfaithful and had deserted her, and to her, spending Christmas alone, deserted and unloved, was almost more than she could bear. And one of the greatest of all of our life's responsibilities for young and old or for rich and poor is to learn how to make a good home.

The reason that God sends parents into the world ahead of their children is so that they can prepare themselves with an education and learn how to make a living and to build up within themselves the right kind of attitudes and faith to be good home-makers. Parents are also given the time to learn to love and appreciate each other. When God said that we should "multiply and replenish the earth," he had some wonderful things in mind. He did not have in mind that home should be merely an address or a place to sleep or a place from which we depart early in the morning and come back too late at night. Home is the very center of all good things.

In 1825 John Howard Payne wrote his famous musical masterpiece, entitled "Home, Sweet Home." When this great poem was written, John Howard Payne was living in Paris, far away from the old homestead that he knew and loved so well. But John Howard Payne was going home. John Howard Payne was going home for a holiday, and John Howard Payne knew that the happiest holidays are those that you go home for. Home is where mother and father are. Home is where you were brought up. Home is where our fondest memories are centered. And John Howard Payne was going home. As he contemplated this coming experience he wrote:

> 'Mid pleasures and palaces though we may roam,
> Be it ever so humble, there's no place like home;
> A charm from the sky seems to hallow us there,
> Which, sought through the world, is ne'er met with elsewhere.
>
> Home, home, sweet, sweet home!
> There's no place like home, oh, there's no place like home!
>
> An exile from home, splendor dazzles in vain;
> Oh, give me my lowly thatched cottage again!
> The birds singing gayly, that came at my call—
> Give me them—and the peace of mind, dearer than all!

However, it has often been pointed out that our lives upon this earth are very brief, and someone has said, "Seeing we are here but for a day's abode, we must look elsewhere for an eternal resting place, where eternity is the measure, felicity is the state, angels are the company, the Lamb is the light, and God is the portion and inheritance."

We have come here to this earth for the most important purposes. But the final objective of our lives is in our heavenly home with God, angels, and our family. And when at Christmastime we are enjoying our homes the most, it might be a pretty good idea to include as a part of our Christmas festivities some contemplation and some planning about how we can most effectively fit ourselves for those mansions in heaven, which the Lord held up as our final objective. Jesus, whose birth we commemorate, has done many wonderful things for us. He has paid the price of our sins and he has made our eternal exaltation possible on condition of our own righteousness. And we might try to imagine what it may sometime be like to commemorate the birth of the Son of God in our Father's house.

Someone has said, "If God has made this earth so fair where sin and death abound, how beautiful beyond compare may paradise be found." If we are true and faithful to him whose birth we celebrate, then someday we will be living where our Heavenly parents are, and what a homecoming that will be!

The account of creation tells us about a period before this earth was formed when we were created by God and lived with him in heaven. It is interesting that all things, including men and women, were created in heaven before they were naturally upon the earth. Our real home is still in heaven. We have all seen God. He is our Father. We lived with him. Then we walked by sight. In the grand council in heaven we were told that this wonderful earth was being created for our mortal benefit. We were told that when we came here we would receive these beautiful, wonderful mortal bodies without which we could never have a fulness of joy, either here or hereafter. And while we knew that because of our free agency this earth would be a place of many problems, yet we also knew that the eternal bodily resurrection would be instituted and that it would be possible for us to return to our heavenly home and live forever with God.

We remember Hans Christian Andersen's story of Gretchen, the poor little match girl. Her mother had died, and for a time she had lived with a wonderful grandmother, but then she had also died. Now she had no real home because her father, with whom she lived, was drunken and cruel. She sold matches in an attempt to keep herself alive. On one bitter cold day during the Christmas season, she had sold no matches all day. She walked the streets in scanty clothing, her feet were blue with cold, and she was faint from hunger. She did not dare go home, and so near midnight she sat down between two protecting buildings in an attempt to warm herself. She thought of the Christchild being born in the stable in Bethlehem. Thoughts of Jesus always gave little Gretchen feelings of comfort and kinship with him as she remembered that the Christchild had also been poor.

Gretchen began to light some of her matches to keep herself warm, and each time while the glow lasted she saw some beautiful Christmas visions of warm fires, good food, comfort, and plenty that cheered her heart, but each time, when the matches went out, the happy visions disappeared. Then she saw a star fall and she knew that someone was dying, although she didn't know that she was the one.

Then Gretchen lighted a big bundle of matches, and in their lighted glow she saw her wonderful grandmother. "Grandmother," she cried, "take me with you, for I know that, like the warm fire, the delicious roast goose, and the beautiful Christmas tree, you will also go away when the matches are burned out." Then in order to prolong her grandmother's stay, she hastily struck all of her matches at once. They blazed with a glow that seemed brighter than day. Her grandmother had never before seemed so beautiful, so gracious, and so loving. Then she lifted little Gretchen into her arms, and in the warm brightness and supreme joy of being together, they flew far away to a beautiful place where there was no cold, or hunger, or fear. In that beautiful place everyone was warm, happy, comfortable, and well provided for, for they were at home with God.

When the cold morning dawned, neighbors found the little match girl in her scant and tattered garments, frozen to death, between the buildings. She sat there facing the wall. Her cheeks were filled with roses and a beautiful smile was on her face. They saw her burned-out matches and said, "She tried to warm herself." As they lifted her up, they shuddered and exclaimed, "It was a bitter, bitter night." It was, of course, impossible for them to know what beauty she had seen, and in what brightness she had gone with her grandmother into the joys of her heavenly home. Neither did they know how much happiness there can sometimes be in a world of misery.

Mr. Andersen's delightful Christmas story might again remind us that the most important objective of this life is to get safely back home for the Christmas of our lives where, like little Gretchen, we can be at peace with our family and God.

The other day I heard an aviator tell about the training he received that was designed to teach him how to fly by his instruments. The instructor would make it so the student couldn't see out of the aircraft. The instructor would fly in all directions in order to get the trainee hopelessly lost and confused. Then he would turn the controls of the aircraft over to the trainee and say to him, "Now take us home. Take us back to the base and land us safely on the ground." This is essentially what we do during our lives. The aviator trainee told about how he would have to learn to find the radar beam and then to stay on it until he was back in the home base.

We think that radar beams are wonderful, and so they are. Radar is one of those great inventions that God has provided for our use. But centuries before the radar beam was discovered, God had put a kind of radar instinct into many of his creatures. We know what he has done for homing pigeons. He has also installed a wonderful device in other birds, enabling them to anticipate the winter's cold and find their way to their southern homes. It is this same gift that enables fish to find their way about in a vast ocean and then accurately get back safely to the spawning grounds where they were born. God has given some wonderful radar equipment to the honeybee that enables the most inexperienced worker bee to know where the sweetest flowers are and then this God-given, unerring instinct will take it directly back to the hive.

But God has given the greatest of all homing instincts to his own children. After each day's work we come home for food and rest to receive the encouragement and the love of those most near and dear to us. We come home for the best part of our education, our inspiration, and a large part of our worship. We want to be home for Christmas. And as a part of our radar equipment, Jesus said, "Follow me." And we make the most and the best of our lives by following his radar beam each day. Then when we have finished with this life, he will take us back to our heavenly home. This is a place where we can spend our eternal lives with God and our families.

This trip back home is not a complicated journey if we follow that straight and narrow way that leads to eternal life. All we need to do is to stay on the beam. And one of the reasons for commemorating Christmas is to get the spirit and fly by the signals that come from his life. He has indicated that we should live by every word that cometh forth from the mouth of God. When we do this, we can safely ride the beam to a most glorious destination and we may make it home for that beautiful Christmastime of our eternal lives. Then we may sing with John Howard Payne, "There is no place like home."

The Lamplighter

S IR HARRY LAUDER used to love to tell the story of the old lamplighter who worked in the small community where he lived as a boy. Each evening as dusk came on, the old man would make his rounds with his ladder and his light. He would put the ladder up against the light post, climb up and light the lamp, step back down, pick up the ladder, and proceed on to the next lamp.

"After a while," said Sir Harry, "the lamplighter would be out of sight down the street, but I could always tell where he had gone because of the lamps he had lighted."

This story of the lamplighter has a great deal in common with our commemoration of Christmas, for among the chief characteristics of Christmas are our Christmas lights. We usually install a community Christmas tree and cover it with beautiful lights. We light our streets, our business buildings, and our churches. We decorate our homes inside and out. And frequently one of the most important community events is when we turn on the Christmas lights.

In memory this might take us back to that earliest morning of creation when the earth "was without form, and void; and darkness was upon the face of the deep." (Genesis 1:2.) Then we might try to understand the transformation when the Spirit of God moved upon the face of the waters. And our creation took its greatest step forward when our world's lights were turned on and God said, "Let there be light." Then that brooding unbroken darkness was pushed back from our earth. The banishment of darkness was also the primary purpose for which the Son of God came to the earth. He came to turn on the lights and put the light of life and love and faith and righteousness into the hearts and minds of God's children.

Dr. Edward Rosenow, formerly of the Mayo Clinic in Rochester, Minnesota, once told of the experience that caused him to choose the field of medicine as his life's work. When Edward was a small boy living in Minnesota, his brother became acutely ill.

The family suffered severe distress until the doctor arrived. As the physician worked over his sick brother, Edward stood behind the doctor with his eye riveted upon the anxious and anguished faces of his parents. Finally the doctor turned to the parents with a smile and said, "You can stop worrying now, for your boy is going to be all right."

Young Edward was profoundly impressed with the change that the announcement made in the faces of his parents. Years later, in relating the incident, he said, "I resolved right then and there that I was going to be a doctor so that I could also go around putting light in people's faces." From that moment, both as a physician and as a man, Dr. Edward Rosenow became a lamplighter.

And the greatest lamplighter who ever lived was also the greatest physician and the greatest man. He not only healed their physical bodies, but he also put the light of hope into their lives. He redeemed all of us from death and made it possible for us to qualify for celestial glory in the city of eternal light.

Some twenty-two centuries before his mortal birth in Bethlehem, he lighted the barges of the Jaredites, enabling them to have light in darkness as they sailed from the Eastern to the Western hemisphere. Inasmuch as the barges would sometimes be submerged in the sea, they had to have some of the features of a submarine. The great prophet, known as the Brother of Jared, had the spirit and the faith of a lamplighter, and because he didn't want to make this long, difficult trip in darkness, he prepared sixteen clear, white transparent stones to give them light. Then he said to the Lord:

"And I know, O Lord, that thou hast all power, and can do whatsoever thou wilt for the benefit of man; therefore touch these stones, O Lord, with thy finger, and prepare them that they may shine forth in darkness; and they shall shine forth unto us in the vessels which we have prepared, that we may have light while we shall cross the sea." (Ether 3:4.)

In answer to the prophet's faith, the Lord stretched forth his hand and touched the stones one by one with his finger, and the stones became luminous as the prophet had requested.

This might remind us of that earlier experience when the Spirit of God moved upon the face of the waters to dispense that brooding, unbroken darkness which covered creation. And according to our faith and works, the Spirit of God may move upon human lives in such a way as to push back that mental darkness of ignorance and to remove the moral blackness of weakness and sin.

Paul refers to the wicked people of his day as the children of darkness. To be enveloped by an oppressive physical night is bad enough, but our most vexing problems arise when darkness gets into our minds or lays its withering hands upon our souls. Isaiah foresaw the approach of the blackness in that awful apostasy from God which brought the Dark Ages upon the world. Of this he said, "Darkness shall cover the earth, and gross darkness the people." Our Eternal Heavenly Father is the God of light, and when we insist on developing that black, sinister condition within ourselves, we separate ourselves from God. And when, by our sins, we say "Let there be darkness," our lives are cut off by hopelessness and despair. All kinds of disobedience have an affinity for evil and flourish most readily in the dark. At the end of each day as the physical light fades from the world, the dens of evil open their doors a little wider. And in all of its many aspects the word *darkness* literally means the absence of light. (Matthew 27:45.)

God uses this word *darkness* as the symbol of sin, denoting the lack of righteousness, intelligence, and life. This word *darkness* has also been used to stand for that dreadful condition called the second death, which comes to people after the powers of evil have gained complete control of the lives of those involved. When our lives are so filled with evil that only sin can flourish, then the possibility for repentance is made so difficult that decency and godliness die and we are left in the dark. Then he that is filthy shall be filthy still and those who are thus affected shall be banished into outer darkness.

One of the most important purposes for which the Savior of the world was born was to lift up those shades of ignorance, atheism, and evil. He came into the world that we might have the light of life and have it more abundantly. But this abundant life is not possible while our deeds keep us living in the dark. The finest progress is brought about when we keep the sunlight of truth and righteousness shining in our lives. We can use our intelligence and industry to roll back the boundaries of ignorance, kill the germs of evil, light the lamps of righteousness, and put the spark of happiness into human lives.

The apostle John speaks of the lamplighting ability of the word of God by saying, "In the beginning was the Word, and the Word was with God, and the Word was God. The same was in the beginning with God. All things were made by him; and without him was not any thing made that was made. In him was life; and the life was the light of men." (John 1:1-4.) He says: "There was a man sent from God, whose name was John. The same came for a witness, to bear witness of the Light, that all men through him might believe. He was not that Light, but was sent to bear witness of that Light. That was the true Light, which lighteth every man that cometh into the world. . . . But as many as received him, to them gave he power to become the sons of God. . . ." (John 1:6-9, 12.)

In this connection Jesus identified his own mission by saying, "I am the light of the world: he that followeth me shall not walk in darkness, but shall have the light of life." (John 8:12.) The Master gave us many important reasons for being afraid of dark deeds. He said: "But if thine eye be evil, thy whole body shall be filled with darkness. . . ." (Matthew 6:23.) And by our own evil we cast ourselves into outer darkness.

God himself lives in light, and if our lives are lighted by his, we may live there also. And because the light of God kills the germs of sin and evil, God has appointed light-bearers, and it becomes our job to assist him in pushing back the darkness on all fronts.

And the writer of Proverbs gives us a helpful figure of speech for our lamplighting abilities when he said: "The spirit of man is the candle of the Lord. . . ." (Proverbs 20:27.) And Jesus gave us this same commission when he said to his disciples: "Ye are the light of the world. A city that is set on a hill cannot be hid. Neither do men light a candle, and put it under a bushel, but on a candlestick; and it giveth light unto all that are in the house. Let your light so shine before men, that they may see your good works, and glorify your Father which is in heaven." (Matthew 5:14-16.)

Our primary function is to assist in lighting the lights of intelligence, righteousness, and understanding in everyone. Then, just as the sun's rays reach out across the world, so the light of Christ will banish darkness and destroy evil and put the light of health, the light of faith, and the light of spirituality in each of us who serve as candles of the Lord. George Washington was a lamplighter. He pushed back the darkness of political bondage and lighted our entire land with liberty and independence. Abraham Lincoln was a lamplighter. In his heart he heard that divine command saying, "Let there be light." And so he devoted his life to that end. Under his stimulating leadership the darkness of human slavery was abolished in our country and he opened the way for equality, opportunity, and human dignity among all men. The light that he lighted still shines forth in a free America and must go on increasing as we get that saving light from God. Then we can say with the psalmist: "Thy word is a lamp unto my feet, and a light unto my path." (Psalm 119:105.)

And so at Christmastime we turn on the lights. We light our homes, we light our Christmas trees, and we light our spirits with that great eternal light. And then as we look at the candles on our Christmas trees and remember the purpose of the birth in Bethlehem, we are reminded that we are candles of the Lord, and that our greatest opportunity is the fulfillment of that great command saying, "Let there be light."

One Empty Stocking

W<small>E HAVE MANY</small> interesting customs with which we commemorate the Christmas season. In our homes we set up Christmas trees decorated with ornaments and lighted with color. We sing beautiful Christmas carols and enjoy the feasting and festive spirit prevailing during this wonderful holiday season. Of course, no Christmas is complete without Santa Claus, sleigh bells, new toys for the children, and presents for everyone.

One of the most interesting of our Christmas customs is to hang up our stockings on Christmas Eve and then go to bed anticipating the morning when we expect to find them bulging with presents.

I know of one family that took great pleasure in designing their own Christmas stockings. They made them from rich, beautiful Christmas material in Christmas colors. The first name of each family member is ornamented on the stocking. Before going to bed they always gather around the fire blazing in the grate. In this happy environment they sing Christmas carols, enjoying their closeness to each other and the love they feel for God. The day is closed with a family prayer in which they kneel and express appreciation and gratitude to their Heavenly Father for their many blessings, including each other.

A home can present an inspiring picture on Christmas Eve with love in the air and Christmas stockings hanging on both sides of the fireplace, waiting to receive the presents that members of the family will give to each other. And what symbol could be more expressive of the spirit of giving and receiving? The Christmas stocking may also serve as an emblem of one's love of family as well as of his love of God.

A symbol is one of the most effective ways of representing things to our minds and emotions. Symbols often make events more memorable. A symbol may be important for itself alone, but it is often even more important for what it stands for and what it gets us to feel and think about. The significance of a ring on the finger or a flag in the sky or a light in the window may go far beyond the importance of the object itself. And a filled Christmas stocking might well represent our compliance with that great command wherein Jesus said, "Love one another."

In a happy home at Christmas time we see a reenactment of that spirit of giving which brought the magi out of the East. Giving is such a wonderfully important part of the Christmas spirit; it is also a wonderfully important part of the spirit of worship and the spirit of service and the spirit of life Itself. Paul, the apostle, in quoting Jesus, said to the elders of Ephesus, "It is more blessed to give than to receive." (Acts 20:35.) It is also more fun and does a lot more good.

William James, the famous psychologist, points to one of our Christmas activities when he reminds us that the deepest hunger in human beings is to be appreciated and loved and made to feel worthwhile. The appropriate giving and receiving of gifts and of the kindness and love that they stimulate feed the soul of the giver as well as the receiver. We can imagine what a terrible ache might be left in our hearts if one family member were forgotten or shunned or left out in the cold at this particular season. The most devastating of all human emotions is that sense of not being wanted, of not belonging, of being excluded and left alone. With this idea in mind, I would like to refer to that ancient story of "The One Empty Stocking."

It wasn't that anyone had really been forgotten. No child had been slighted or made unhappy, and no adult had been left unremembered. The presents had been distributed and all of the stockings were bountifully and beautifully filled—all, that is, except one; there was one stocking that had never even been hung up. It was the stocking intended for the Child of Bethlehem. Of all of the people belonging at that Christmas fireside, only *he* had been forgotten, only he had been left out of the festivities. This didn't seem quite right, inasmuch as it was *his* birthday that was being celebrated.

This interesting story of forgetfulness and neglect reminds us of the many times that such an oversight has occurred. His birth into the world was important enough to draw a great multitude of the host of heaven from the very presence of God out through space to the hills of Bethlehem. Yet except for the stable, there was no room for the Christ child to be born. "No room" was a continuing theme throughout the entire mortal life of the Son of God. And the very people whom he came to redeem from death have reenacted over and over again this ancient scene at the inn, in which no room could be found for the honored guest.

Jesus was sent to the earth to lead us to celestial glory. But instead of following him, the world he came to save has so filled itself with evil that it has left no room for his righteousness. We have made room for his gifts, but often no room has been found for the giver. Many people make room for sports and recreation on the Sabbath day but make no room for worship or Christian service.

The fact that someone has been slighted previously does not make future slights easier to bear. Sometimes our hearts get more tender with each succeeding hurt. We are shamed by the circumstances that forced upon Jesus the long string of indignities during his life which finally led to his shameful death, but to date these conditions have not been greatly improved. Certainly the peace and righteousness about which the angels sang were never farther away than now, nor has our appreciation of his life greatly increased.

At Christmastime we would be very grateful for gifts of automobiles or houses or lands, but what have we done in appreciation of him who has given us the entire earth with all of its beauty, abundance, and opportunity? Or how do we regard him who gave us the gifts of life and health and love and ability and personality and the promise of eternal life?

Christmas is noted primarily for its gifts, and every good gift comes from God. For weeks before Christmas we devote ourselves to our shopping. We try to decide what we can get for each member of our family and each of our friends. But the best Christmas gifts are not found in the stores or under the Christmas tree. The best gifts are in the lives of people. When one of our children was very small, he obtained a present for me at a substantial sacrifice to himself. Then in his childish, scrawling hand, he wrote me a letter in which he poured out the affection of his loving, childish heart. What a wealth of joy the spirit of such a present brings. I have kept his letter ever since and it becomes more precious as the years go by. Each time I read it, it renews in my heart a feeling that closely approaches worship. Emerson said, "Rings and jewels are not gifts but apologies for gifts. The only true gift is a portion of thyself."

My son's present was of himself; it was only represented by the gift. His letter reminds me over and over again that I also have some things to give that are not available in the store. As a usual thing we give presents to those who have previously given presents to us. But our most worthwhile presents have always come from him whose birth we celebrate. What a thrill it should be to us at the Christmas season to place a substantial gift in that stocking that has been empty for such a long time.

Again we might go through the process of saying, "What can I give?" It may seem to us that *he* also has everything. But there is something that he may not have which he greatly desires, the giving of which will both please him and enrich us. Above all things God desires an upright heart in his children. The greatest gift that our children can give us is their lives filled with devotion, honor, love, and an expansion of their own godly personal endowments. And that is the way that we can most please God.

Through the prophet Micah it was said, "He hath shewed thee, O man, what is good"; then he asks, "and what doth the Lord require of thee, but to do justly, to love mercy, and to walk humbly with thy God?" (Micah 6:8.)

As our deepest hungers are to be loved, so God's two greatest commandments have to do with loving God and righteously serving our fellowmen. Christ was born at Bethlehem, and the best in us may be born on his birthday, as we fill the empty stocking with those gifts that he most greatly appreciates.

Suppose, therefore, at this Christmas season we reestablish the pattern set by the wise men and give a present to Jesus, one that will make him happy and at the same time will exalt and ennoble us. In this way, as we commemorate his birth, *we* will be born again in harmony with the best possible meaning of his own command.

The Life of Christ

ONE OF THE greatest opportunities for bringing about the growth of our human understanding is found in the study of biography. By knowing what others have done, we may get better acquainted with that mysterious primal element called life in which all of us have our being and from which all of our human experience is fashioned. Life is the most valuable commodity in the universe. It also offers the most profitable opportunity for our own research and development. An actual access to a knowledge of the greatest men is almost impossible during their lifetime. The kind of people who can help us most are very busy and are usually separated from us by the serious barriers of time and space. But through biography the most humble of us can have as many contacts as we like with the greatest men in any field. This contact may have a limitless diversity and may be made on our own terms. This is a privilege granted to us which those people living at the same time and in the same community with great men could never hope to enjoy.

The biographies of great men give us many advantages over those who lived contemporaneously with them. We can see both the causes and the consequences of their failures and successes. Think how much benefit has already come from reading the lives of George Washington and Abraham Lincoln. Alexander the Great left his living schoolmaster Aristotle behind him, but he took the works of dead Homer with him. And it is said that Alexander developed more bravery by reading Homer's "Life of Achilles" than anything that he could have learned from Aristotle about the definitions of fortitude. The delights of biography are among the greatest in all of our human relationships. The association and stimulation of great people shed upon us a peculiar satisfaction. The study of biography is a sort of detective work in which we shadow destiny itself and we are not restricted to explore only the surface of their lives, but we may dive into its depths and measure its breadths as well.

When we study the biographies of great people, we soon feel

a new life moving within ourselves. Biographies cause new ambitions and new aspirations to incarnate themselves in our own personalities. And we may avail ourselves of all men's faculties and virtues.

Benjamin Franklin's autobiography was written in his seventy-ninth year and was directed toward his son. Then for the balance of his son's life he could re-read his father's words and hear his father talk to him about the interesting details of his own success. And what father would not like to talk on this most favorable basis to his own children and grandchildren? What a delight it would be if we could make ourselves always available to take our children on a tour of our own lives and point out to them some of the things that we have learned in our own most valuable experiences. It may be much more helpful if we could go with them through the great literature and point out the highest values in human virtues and ideas. This was one of the ambitions of God himself when he caused the holy scriptures to be written. They are filled with the best ideas and activities and are loaded with the most inspiring things about the great universal Father himself.

Somebody has said that the holy scripture is a kind of God's *Who's Who*. It tells us many things about the people who are important to God, and the most profitable biography with which we could concern ourselves is with him whose birth we commemorate at this season of the year. Jesus said, "And this is life eternal, that they might know thee the only true God, and Jesus Christ, whom thou hast sent." (John 17:3.) The greatest responsibility that is ever placed upon the shoulders of any human being is to know God and what the divine purpose for us is. To this end we set apart this special season of the year, during which we commemorate the birth of Christ, and it can be very profitable for us to know as much as possible about him. There are literally hundreds of prophecies in the Old Testament about the Son of God. And he is also the very center and substance of the New Testament.

Most great biographies begin on the day of one's birth, but to understand the life of Christ we need a much earlier beginning date. Nothing is more plainly written in the scripture than the fact that the life of Christ did not begin at Bethlehem, neither did it end on Calvary. It is just as certain that our lives did not begin when we were born, neither will they end when we die. Of himself, Jesus said, "I came forth from the Father, and am come into the world: again, I leave the world, and go to the Father." (John 16:28.) In his great intercessory prayer he said to his father, "Neither pray I for these alone, but for them also which shall believe on me through their word; That they all may be one; as thou, Father, art in me, and I in thee, that they also may be one in us: that the world may believe that thou hast sent me." (John 17:20-21.)

He said, "And now, O Father, glorify thou me with thine own self with the glory which I had with thee before the world was." (John 17:5.) The scripture is perfectly clear about the fact that all of the people, including Christ, who have ever lived upon this earth are the spirit children of God. We were all begotten by him in an antemortal state long before this earth was created. Our lives are so closely connected with the life of Christ that they can best be studied together.

Jesus Christ was the First Begotten in the spirit and the most capable of God's children. (Romans 8:29.) For ages before this earth was created, he lived and ruled with his Father in heaven where the creations of this earth first took place on a spiritual basis. (See Genesis 2:5.)

In some other writings of Moses not found in the Bible the Lord further says, "And worlds without number have I created; and I also created them for mine own purpose; and by the Son I created them, which is mine only begotten." (Moses 1:33.)

In trying to help us understand our own situation, somebody has compared our lives to a three-act play. There was a long antemortal existence, which was our first act. Then we have a little short mortality, which is our second act. And we look forward to an eternal, everlasting third act. And someone has said that if we were to go into the theater after the first act had been finished and left before the third act began, we may not understand the play.

Some 2,000 years before his birth in Bethlehem, the antemortal Christ revealed himself and explained something of his situation to a great prophet known in the Book of Mormon as the Brother of Jared. And he said to him, "Behold, this body, which you now behold, is the body of my spirit; and man have I created after the body of my spirit; and even as I appear unto thee to be in the spirit will I appear unto my people in the flesh." (Ether 3:16.)

When the biography of any person is written, we usually want to know what he has done for his fellowmen. For countless ages, Jesus Christ was known as Jehovah and was associated with his Father Elohim in the presidency of heaven. Christ had much to do with our training and development during those long ante-mortal years. Under the direction of his Father he was the Creator of this earth and accepted the appointment to come here and be its Redeemer. His coming birth was announced more than 1970 years ago when a heavenly messenger of great authority and power was sent from God to a young woman living in Galilee by the name of Mary, to announce that she had been selected to be the mother of the Son of God.

During his ministry in the meridian of time, Jesus organized his Church with the direction that everyone should belong to it. He said to his apostles: "Go ye into all the world, and preach the gospel to every creature. He that believeth and is baptized shall be saved; but he that believeth not shall be damned." (Mark 16:15-16.)

He taught to the world those great principles of the gospel on which our eternal exaltation depends. He took upon himself our sins and became our Redeemer by giving his life for us. By long odds he is the greatest man who ever lived. But one of the most serious mistakes that anyone could ever make is to assume that Jesus was just a great teacher or a great humanitarian. He is also God.

It is wonderful to recount the traditions of the wise men, the Bethlehem star, the account of the shepherds, the angelic chorus, and Jesus' humble birth in the manger. But we should also remember that he is the Son of God, the Savior of the World, and the Redeemer of men. And the greatest good fortune that we could bring about in our lives would be to accept his doctrines and govern our lives according to his teachings.

Many years ago Dr. Henry C. Link wrote a great book entitled *The Return to Religion.* Dr. Link had grown up in a religious household, but as he climbed the educational ladder he decided that he might make a more intellectual approach to life through his education, and so he relaxed somewhat his hold on his religious convictions. But at age thirty-two, with his Phi Beta Kappa key on his chest and his name in *Who's Who in America,* he became the head of the Psychological Service Center of New York City, where it was his responsibility to advise thousands of troubled people how to best solve their problems. Then Dr. Link made an important discovery that we should also make. He discovered that we can best solve all of our problems by a return to the religion of Christ. That is, just think how it would transform our world if everyone obeyed the Ten Commandments and the Sermon on the Mount and every other direction that he has given.

We not only know a great many of the facts in the life of Christ that have already passed, but we also know a great deal about what his future life will be and how we will be affected by it. We know that the time is getting very close when he will come to this earth in power and great glory to cleanse it of its wickedness and to begin that tremendous period when he will personally reign for a thousand years upon the earth. This will be that period of time when the designated work of this earth will be completed. The family of God will be given its final education and training in preparation for that other tremendous event, the final judgment. Then this earth will be elevated in its status to a celestial sphere, and those upon this earth who have qualified for celestial glory will inherit it. We need to accept with great enthusiasm every one of his teachings.

The most important idea that there is in the world is that God lives, that he is our Father, that Jesus Christ is our Savior and Redeemer, and that our obedience to the gospel of Christ is all-important. In reflecting my own witness, I would like to borrow some words written by Lewis D. Edwards, who said:

> I know that my Redeemer lives;
> What comfort this sweet sentence gives!
> He lives, he lives, who once was dead.
> He lives, my ever-living head.
> He lives to bless me with his love.
> He lives to plead for me above.
> He lives my hungry soul to feed.
> He lives to bless in time of need.

He lives to grant me rich supply,
He lives to guide me with his eye.
He lives to comfort me when faint.
He lives to hear my soul's complaint.
He lives to silence all my fears.
He lives to wipe away my tears.
He lives to calm my troubled heart.
He lives, all blessings to impart.

He lives, my kind, wise, heav'nly friend.
He lives and loves me to the end.
He lives, and while he lives, I'll sing,
He lives, my Prophet, Priest and King.
He lives and grants me daily breath.
He lives, and I shall conquer death.
He lives my mansion to prepare.
He lives to bring me safely there.

He lives, all glory to his name!
He lives, my savior, still the same;
O sweet the joy this sentence gives:
"I know that my Redeemer lives!"

May God bless us all so to know and so to do is my humble Christmas prayer.

The Useful Fiction of Christmas

IT IS INTERESTING to contemplate that a very large part of the great literature of our world comes under the heading of useful fiction. The dictionary says that fiction is that class of knowledge which is invented or imagined. Of course there is a harmful fiction, the purpose of which is to deceive or to destroy. However, there is a great useful fiction, the purpose of which is to build us up, increase our ability, and make us more successful and happy.

Our great literary fiction is made up of stories, dramas, parables, and myths. There is a moral fiction, a romantic fiction, and a fiction involving the principles of success.

Some 600 years B.C. a great man by the name of Aesop wrote a large collection of helpful fables. He gave character qualities, personality traits, and words of wisdom to animals, and then he had them act out some great truths for our benefit. And while many of the events described may have never happened in actual fact, yet they could have happened and the principles involved may be even more true and more helpful than if they had actually happened many times. That is, we can still learn a great deal from the old fable of the tortoise and the hare, the lion and the mouse, the fox and the grapes. We have the interesting comparisons and parables of the scriptures that teach us truths that would be difficult to get in any other way.

Solomon said, "Go to the ant, thou sluggard; consider her ways, and be wise." (Proverbs 6:6.) In the thirteenth chapter of Matthew, Jesus compared the kingdom of heaven with six things, all of which were completely different and yet therein some great truths are made crystal clear. And Mark says that without a parable Jesus spake naught unto the people. Jesus himself always seemed to be alert for new and useful comparisons. On one occasion he said, "Unto what should I liken this generation?" It is not necessary that the parable of the sower or the mustard seed or the unprofitable servant or the wheat and the tares or the pearl of great price actually happened as they were given in each specific case, and yet these great stories are among the great treasures of our literature. They are very helpful in building up our own philosophy. It would be very unfortunate for us if we had to wait until every great idea had actually been materialized in some specific action before we could profit from it.

Frequently in the actual experience we find the good and the bad, the pleasant and the unpleasant mixed up together. But in our stories and our comparisons we can separate the sheep from the goats and use only the uplifting, the inspiring, and the pleasant. Thus we can be made richer without being made poorer at the same time.

Much of our greatest literature is centered in Christmas. Christmas is not only our most important day; it is also our most uplifting and should be our most pleasant. And at the Christmas season we recount the great factual events that are necessary in God's program for our eternal welfare, but then over the years in various parts of the world, people have added color, pleasure, and interest with many such things as our Christmas feasting and other festivities.

In our art, drama, and music we tell of the beautiful Bethlehem star and sing songs about the three kings that came from the East bearing the first Christmas gifts. And on our Christmas cards we picture these great men and their camels in beautiful robes and wonderful color in contrast to the simple shepherds in their humble garb tending their flocks upon the Judean hills.

Then we have this wonderful influence of Santa Claus, who makes such an important contribution to Christmas for so many people. And while it is customary to regard the story of Santa Claus as a myth, yet he is the result of a kind of evolution from the legend of a real person who lived during the fourth century who was called St. Nicholas. Nicholas was the only child of wealthy Christian parents and was born at the close of the third century, perhaps about 280, at Patara, a port in the providence of Lycia in Asia Minor. Early in his childhood his devout mother taught him the scripture. When both parents died during an epidemic, they left the young boy in possession of all of their wealth.

Young Nicholas dedicated his life to God's service and moved to Myra, chief city of his province, and was appointed to be their bishop. Because of his youth he tried to refuse the position, but he was overruled. On one occasion, Nicholas learned of three young women who had no suitors because their father was too poor to provide them with a dowry, so one night he filled three bags with gold and threw them into the windows of the rooms occupied by the young women, and they soon were happily married. Thereafter unexpected gifts were said to come from St. Nicholas. In the course of time, he came to be described as the giver of Christmas presents. The children put their shoes and stockings beside the fireplace on Christmas Eve in the hopes that St. Nicholas would fill them with presents. St. Nicholas was naturally a very happy person and was eventually called "Jolly old St. Nicholas." We sing songs about him and think of him as the one who rewards the good deeds of others. Someone has written:

> Jolly old St. Nicholas,
> Lean your ear this way.
> Don't you tell a single soul
> What I'm going to say,
> Christmas eve is coming soon,
> Now you dear old man,
> Whisper what you'll bring to me,
> Tell me if you can.
>
> Johnny wants a pair of skates,
> Susie wants a dolly,
> Mary wants a story book,
> She thinks dolls are folly.
> As for me, my little brain
> Is not very bright.
> Choose for me dear Santa Claus
> What you think is right.

When we identify with this jolly, happy, generous person of Santa Claus, we tend to adopt his many virtues. And in our presents and carols, etc. we are following the suggestion of David when he said, "Make a joyful noise to the Lord." And many of our songwriters have set our Christmas messages to music. Indeed, the word *carol* implies the jovial retelling of the story of some serious subject.

Dr. Clement Clarke Moore, a professor in the General Theological Seminary in New York, put one of the light messages of Christmas and Santa Claus into verse under the title of "The Visit of St. Nicholas." It is said that Dr. Moore invented the sleigh and the reindeer of Santa Claus. And his description of St. Nicholas was suggested by the appearance of a German handyman who was in his employ. The sleighbells were suggested by the bells on his own horse as he was driving home on a winter evening. He wrote the poem in 1822 for his own children and read it to them on the Christmas Eve in that year. It says:

'Twas the night before Christmas when all through the house,
Not a creature was stirring, not even a mouse;
The stockings were hung by the chimney with care,
In hopes that St. Nicholas soon would be there;
The children were nestled all snug in their beds,
While visions of sugar-plums danced in their heads;
And Mamma in her kerchief, and I in my cap
Had just settled down for a long winter's nap,
When out on the lawn there arose such a clatter,
I sprang from my bed to see what was the matter.
Away to the window I flew like a flash,
Tore open the shutters and pulled up the sash.
The moon on the breast of the new-fallen snow
Gave a luster of mid-day to objects below;
When, what to my wandering eyes should appear,
But a miniature sleigh, and eight tiny reindeer,
With a little old driver, so lively and quick,
I knew in a moment it must be St. Nick.
More rapid than eagles, his coursers they came,
And he whistled, and shouted, and called them by name:
"Now, Dasher! now, Dancer! now, Prancer and Vixen!
On, Comet! on, Cupid! on, Donner and Blitzen!
To the top of the porch, to the top of the wall!
Now, Dash away, dash away, dash away, all!"
As dry leaves that before the wild hurricane fly,
When they meet with an obstacle, mount to the sky,
So, up to the house-top the coursers they flew,
With a sleigh full of toys—and St. Nicholas, too.
And then in a twinkle I heard on the roof
The prancing and pawing of each little hoof,
As I drew in my head, and was turning around,
Down the chimney St. Nicholas came with a bound.
He was dressed all in fur from his head to his foot,
And his clothes were all tarnished with ashes and soot;
A bundle of toys he had flung on his back,
And he looked like a peddler just opening his pack.
His eyes how they twinkled! his dimples how merry!
His cheeks were like roses, his nose like a cherry;
His droll little mouth was drawn up like a bow,

And the beard on his chin was as white as the snow.
The stump of a pipe he held tight in his teeth,
And the smoke it encircled his head like a wreath;
He had a broad face and a little round belly
That shook, when he laughed, like a bowlful of jelly.
He was chubby and plump—a right jolly old elf;
And I laughed when I saw him, in spite of myself.
A wink of his eye, and a twist of his head,
Soon gave me to know I had nothing to dread.
He spoke not a word, but went straight to his work,
And filled all the stockings; then turned with a jerk,
And laying his finger aside of his nose,
And giving a nod, up the chimney he rose.
He sprang to his sleigh, to his team gave a whistle,
And away they all flew like the down on a thistle;
But I heard him exclaim, ere he drove out of sight,
"Happy Christmas to all, and to all a goodnight!"

In our own day we have invented an addition to the reindeer team of Santa Claus. Probably the most famous reindeer of all is Rudolph with his shiny red nose. Since 1822 we have known Dasher and Dancer and Prancer and Vixen, Comet, Cupid, Donner, and Blitzen, but now we also have Rudolph, the most famous reindeer of all. And so now we sing:

Rudolph, the red-nosed reindeer,
had a very shiny nose,
And if you ever saw it,
You would even say it glows.

All of the other reindeer
Used to laugh and call him names;
They wouldn't let poor Rudolph
Join in any reindeer games.

Then one foggy Christmas eve,
Santa came to say,
"Rudolph, with your nose so bright,
Won't you guide my sleigh tonight?"

Then, how the reindeer loved him,
And they shouted out with glee,
"Rudolph, the red-nosed reindeer,
You'll go down in history."

We look forward to the beautiful white snow of Christmas and sing:

I'm dreaming of a white Christmas
Just like the ones I used to know,
Where the tree-tops glisten
And children listen
To hear the sleighbells in the snow.

I'm dreaming of a white Christmas
With ev'ry Christmas card I write.
May your days be merry and bright,
And may all your Christmases be white.

Santa Claus may be primarily for children but he is also for all of us. And in one way or another we should keep in mind that Santa Claus is coming to town:

You better watch out, you better not cry
You better not pout, I'm telling you why,
Santa Claus is coming to town.
He's making a list and checking it twice,
Trying to find out who's naughty and nice,
Santa Claus is coming to town.

He sees you when you're sleeping
He knows if you're awake,
He knows if you've been bad or good,
So be good for goodness sake.

You better watch out, you better not cry
You better not pout, I'm telling you why,
Santa Claus is coming to town.

Little children accept the Santa Claus myth without question, but as they grow older they begin to have doubts. One of them in 1897 wrote to the *New York Sun* asking whether there is a Santa Claus. Its answer, written by Francis P. Church and printed as an editorial article, has become almost as famous as Dr. Moore's poem. Here it is:

We take pleasure in answering thus prominently the communication below, expressing at the same time our great gratification that its faithful author is numbered among the friends of the Sun:

Dear Editor—
I am eight years old. Some of my little friends say there is no Santa Claus. Papa says 'If you see it in *The Sun* it's so.' Please tell me the truth, is there a Santa Claus?
                              Virginia O'Hanlon

Virginia, your little friends are wrong. They have been affected by the skepticism of a skeptical age. They do not believe except they see. They think that nothing can be which is not comprehensible by their little minds. All minds, Virginia, whether they be men's or children's, are little. In this great universe of ours man is a mere insect, an ant, in his intellect as compared with the boundless world about him, as measured by the intelligence capable of grasping the whole of truth and knowledge.

Yes, Virginia, there is a Santa Claus. He exists as certainly as love and generosity and devotion exist, and you know that they abound and give to your life its highest beauty and joy. Alas! How dreary would be the world if there were no Santa Claus! It would be as dreary as if there were no Virginias. There would be no childlike faith then, no poetry, no romance to make tolerable this existence. We should have no enjoyment, except in sense and sight. The eternal light with which childhood fills the world would be extinguished.

Not believe in Santa Claus! You might as well not believe in fairies. You might get your papa to hire men to watch in all the chimneys on Christmas eve to catch Santa Claus, but even if you did not see Santa Claus coming down, what would that prove? Nobody sees Santa Claus, but that is no sign that there is no Santa Claus. The most real things in the world are those that neither children nor men can see. Did you ever see fairies dancing on the lawn? Of course not, but that's no proof that they are not there. Nobody can conceive or imagine all the wonders there are unseen and unseeable in the world.

You tear apart the baby's rattle and see what makes the noise inside, but there is a veil covering the unseen world which not the strongest man, nor even the united strength of all the strongest men that ever lived could tear apart. Only faith, poetry, love, romance, can push aside that curtain and view and picture the supernal beauty and glory beyond. Is it all real? Ah, Virginia, in all this world there is nothing else real and abiding.

No Santa Claus! Thank God! He lives and lives forever. A thousand years from now, Virginia, nay, ten times ten thousand years from now, he will continue to make glad the heart of childhood.

The Miracle at the Inn

A T THE CHRISTMAS season we delight to hear over and over again the thrilling stories having to do with the most important event that ever happened upon the earth, the birth of him who was ordained of God to be the Savior of the world.

Many of the great events recorded in the scriptures are given so briefly that many of the important details and interesting sidelights had to be left out. There are single pages in the Bible containing all that is recorded in the history of the world for five hundred years. In our contemplation of some of the great Bible events we may sometimes try to fill in some of the interesting details out of our imagination. For example, isn't it interesting to try to picture the kind of young woman Mary must have been to have been chosen by God to be the mother of this particular Son. What a fascinating insight it would give us if we had more background for these important events.

The announcement of the birth of Jesus was apparently made in various ways to quite a large number of people in various parts of the world, including certain wise men in the East as well as some people living in the western hemisphere, and to the shepherds tending their flocks upon the neighboring Judean hills. We never weary of the thrilling account of these great Christmas stories.

In our imagination it is very interesting to try to fill in some of the more intimate details. The announcement of the birth of Christ was also made to other people who lived at a greater distance from Bethlehem, including wise men from the East. (Matthew 2:1.) Ever since that day when the original wise men followed the star that led them to the manger in Bethlehem, other wise men have also been trying to find the king. And it is small wonder that this should be so, for as Peter says, "Neither is there salvation in any other: for there is none other name under heaven given among men, whereby we must be saved." (Acts 4:12.)

The journey of the wise men was over when they had found the King, and so is ours. His life represents the main objective in our lives. Certainly the worst tragedy of the world of 1900 years ago is that such a large number of people never found the King. That is also the worst tragedy of our day. Our most serious problem is not that men should some time die, but that they should never live in the best sense of the term. God is the source of life. The greatest of all discoveries is when man discovers God, and many people have made this important discovery at Christmastime.

We love the story of the wise men following the star to Bethlehem. We enjoy the legend of the three kings riding their camels out of the East and across the desert to worship Jesus and to offer their service and lay their valuable presents at his feet, but certainly all of those who did great service did not get into the official records.

Many great men and women devote their lives to the service of others and, through no fault of their own, never quite make the headlines.

It was this kind of an idea that prompted the erection of a monument to the unknown soldier. He is a soldier who gave his life for his country, and yet the notice of his heroism was never printed in the newspapers. Most of the great deeds of the world are not done before the eye of the camera, and sometime ago, I heard the story of another "unknown soldier," who did valiant service in connection with the birth of the son of God, that I would like to share with you.

We remember that when Joseph and Mary came to Bethlehem that first Christmas night there was no room found for them in the inn and the Christ child was born in a stable. Again, wouldn't it be interesting if we had a few more of the details surrounding this event in the Lord's life. In the *Christmas News* of December 20, 1947, a prize-winning Christmas story was printed that had been written by Betty Wall Madsen. It was entitled "The Miracle at the Inn." This is the kind of a beautiful experience that frequently happens that we never hear about.

The story centers around a little ten-year-old boy by the name of Haun. Haun was a little crippled boy, the son of Japhet, the innkeeper at Bethlehem. Because of his twisted back and his awkward hump, he was unable to run and play and do the things that other boys did. But Haun was a fine boy, and he was made responsible by his father for the care of the inn stable where the animals were kept. Haun loved animals and he did his work in the stable with great pride and joy. Day after day he faithfully worked at his job to keep the stable clean and make it a pleasant place. Sometimes Haun obtained permission from his parents to sleep in the stable with the animals that he loved. He would put fresh hay in one part of the manger and make himself a comfortable bed. He took such pride in his work in the stable and he loved the animals so that it was a great delight to him when he could sleep in his bed in the manger.

Then tax time came, when many people came crowding into Bethlehem. With all of the activity on this particular day Haun worked very hard as there was much to be done. But Haun also liked to watch the people who came to stay at the inn owned by his father. Long after the inn had been filled, Joseph and Mary came seeking a place to spend the night. While Joseph was talking with Japhet, Haun held the gray donkey on which Mary sat. He loved all animals, but he particularly loved this little donkey. But more than all, he loved the beautiful young woman who was so kind to him as she waited. She asked Haun about himself and Haun told her about his work and the animals that he cared for.

Haun heard his father tell Joseph that they had no room in the inn. He saw the disappointment on Mary's face as she wondered what they would do, where they could go. All of Bethlehem was crowded. Every bed and corner had already been taken.

Haun felt a queer feeling of regret settle in his stomach as he tried to think of some way to help them. As Joseph turned the donkey around and started to leave, little crippled Haun had an idea. What about his bed in the manger? Excitedly he tugged at his father's arm as he told him his plan. When he saw by the expression in his father's face that his father would not object, he ran after Joseph and Mary as best he could until he caught up with them. Then to this kind, friendly lady he offered his bed on the hay in the manger of the stable. Haun must have taken great pride in helping them to get settled and making them comfortable. He gave them his lantern, which was so helpful after dark.

Later that night Haun and his parents were awakened by music and voices. The stable was shining with a beautiful light.

His father said, "Haun, my son, we will go to the stable and see the cause of this strange occurrence. I have never seen such a beautiful light before." Then Haun and his father and mother went quickly to the stable behind the inn. As they walked, Japhet put his arm protectingly across Haun's misshapen shoulders. The stable door stood open. Haun's lantern had been lighted and hung from the rafters, and across the threshold a warm, golden yellow light fell. Joseph stood by the manger, his eyes not tired now. The beautiful lady lay upon Haun's bed of hay and held a baby in her arms. Haun gave an exclamation of surprise. He thought, "My mother is beautiful, but this lady is like light." Then Haun thought, "What a beautiful baby!"

In his great eagerness and haste to get a closer look he fell and sprawled awkwardly upon the stable floor toward the manger. After collecting himself, he reached up and took hold of the side of the manger and pulled himself up until his head rested against the edge of the manger bed. He was usually more humiliated than hurt when his crippled body caused him to fall, as it made him appear awkward in the presence of strangers. This time he held his lips pressed firmly together.

His embarrassment passed quickly, however, as he heard the soft voice of Mary speaking to him, saying, "Haun, I think my little son loves you very much. See, his tiny hand is laid against your head." Then they heard the singing of the angels, and Haun felt an inner feeling that he had never known before. His crippled body arose quickly. He had never before moved with such swiftness, nor had he ever felt as happy. His head was erect; there was joy in his heart. His shadow cast upon the stable wall by the lantern now seemed tall and straight and strong.

The prophets had foretold that Jesus would be born in Bethlehem under very humble circumstances. The Lord had also said something about using the weak in his service. Maybe Haun had been especially selected to provide his clean, comfortable place for the Christchild to be born. How happy he was that he had done his work so well, that the stable was ready and such a pleasant place. It looked so beautiful to Haun now, filled as it was with radiant golden light. These wonderful visitors were really his guests. There was no room for them in the inn and no room anyplace in Bethlehem, but Haun had made room in what to him was the best place of all, the stable among the animals that he loved.

Later the shepherds and others also came to Haun's stable to see the Son of God.

Haun would always remember this wonderful night, but what was more, he would remember his wonderful guests. There would always be room in his heart for the Christ, which God had directed to him. Certainly Haun would always keep his own life clean, pleasant, and worthy. Who knows but that at some later day Haun may again have felt the hand of Jesus upon his head, and who in all of Christ's ministry would be more entitled to hear the Master say, "Well done, thou good and faithful servant; thou hast been faithful over a few things, I will make thee ruler over many things: enter thou into the joy of thy lord." (Matthew 25:21.) May we get the spirit of Christmas and Christian service, not only at Christmas, but at all times throughout our lives.

The Light of the World

MANY YEARS AGO the famous English painter Holman Hunt painted a great religious masterpiece entitled "The Light of the World." The painting is a visualization of that interesting scripture in which Jesus says, "Behold, I stand at the door, and knock: if any man hear my voice, and open the door, I will come in to him, and will sup with him, and he with me." (Revelation 3:20.)

In this painting, Jesus is shown standing outside a firmly shut door in the half light of the evening. He has his right hand upon the door knocker. At his feet weeds have grown tall and rank, indicating that the door had not been opened for a long time. But Jesus stands patiently awaiting a response. His head is haloed like the corona of the harvest moon; his kingly crown is entwined with that other crown of thorns. In his left hand he holds a lantern, which casts a flickering light upon the weeds surrounding the door and also reveals the nail prints in his wounded hands.

When the original of this picture was first exhibited in London, the critics immediately seized the opportunity to say that Mr. Hunt had made an omission in his painting. On the door a knocker was plainly shown, but a handle or doorknob by which the door could be opened had been forgotten. Mr. Hunt explained that many of the doors with which Jesus was familiar had the latch only on the inside and could not be opened from without. By knocking on the outside, one could only make his presence known. His knock could do nothing more than to indicate his desire to be admitted, but the door itself had to be opened from inside.

Even today we have many doors where the one-way locking device is so set that it can only be opened from the inside. Turning the doorknob on the inside readily opens the door. But the outside doorknob is completely useless as a means of gaining admittance, unless the lock is released from the inside. With this device there is created an important religious symbol. It is a well-known fact that the door to one's heart can also be opened most readily from within. I suppose that no one has ever yet forced his way into the affections or love of another person. And above almost everything else, God himself is committed to free agency and love as the governing principles of his program for his children. God never forces us to do right, and Satan has no power to force us to do wrong. Each one only knocks on the outside of the door, and we open it to whomsoever we will.

The motivation of this great scripture and picture is particularly timely at Christmas. This is when we delight most in recounting the thrilling stories connected with the birth of Jesus Christ, who was ordained to be the Savior of the world. In our minds at Christmas time, we again see the new star arising in the east, leading the wise men across the desert to lay their treasures at the feet of the newborn king. We also decorate our homes and give Christmas presents to each other. But one of the most important objectives to be accomplished during the commemoration of his birth is to get the spirit of his life reborn into our own hearts. To be directed by his spirit is the most important of all of the secrets of human success.

It was Jesus himself who said to his followers, "I am the light of the world: he that followeth me shall not walk in darkness, but shall have the light of life." (John 8:12.) John gave this idea in a little different form when he said, "In him was life, and the life was the light of men." It is wonderful to see our homes and Christmas trees beautifully lighted with electricity, but it is even more wonderful and much more important to have human lives illuminated and motivated by him who was ordained to be the Light of the world and to help us get his attitudes into our lives.

Certainly one of our greatest individual Christmas pictures might well be our own visualization of the Light of the world, knocking a little louder at Christmastime at the doors of our hearts. On the night of his birth, there was no room found for him in the inn. But his birth was not the only time during his life that he was excluded by men. For his entire thirty-three years on earth, this cry of "no room" almost became a theme song for his life. With many people there was no room for his teaching. There was no room for his miracles, no room for his doctrines, no room for his faith.

Even in our own day, with the judgment of time shining upon his life, we are still reenacting the ancient scene of Bethlehem by crying, "No room, no room." We make room for the gifts, but often we have no room for the giver. We have room for our own commercialism of Christmas and our pleasure seeking on the Sabbath day, but too often we have no room for worship. No room for service, no room for righteousness. The reason there was no room in the inn was because all of the available space was already occupied. And we are only following the ancients when we fill our lives so full of other things that we have no time or space left for the Light and Life of the world.

One of the most stimulating experiences in life is that which we sometimes have of entertaining some famous person. It is a great delight when some individual of great consequence becomes our guest and honors us by coming into our home to be with us and to share with us his wisdom and friendship. We might just suppose that the mayor, or the governor, or even the president was a very close friend of ours, and that occasionally we were permitted to share in the benefits of his greatness by a close intimate association with him. How we would listen for that knock on the door that would announce his arrival. What a delightful experience it can be to enjoy a good meal with those for whom we have great love and respect. There are some people whose presence makes us glad, and we are wonderfully stimulated by their love and uplifted by their wisdom and encouragement.

While in the presence of some famous person, we listen eagerly to every word that he says. And when he is gone, we talk to our other friends about the experience. We quote him to them, in order that they might also share with us the benefits of his abilities. Merely to read about some famous individual or to receive a letter from him is never quite as stimulating as an actual face-to-face visit. It has been said that no one has ever succeeded in putting a great man down on paper. You may get his ideas, his illustrations, and his words on paper, but you can't get the man. That is, you can't get the smile on his face, or the light in his eye, or the warmth of his handshake, or the love in his voice on the paper. The best way to get the spirit of a great man is by coming into close contact with him personally.

Certainly one of the greatest needs of our personal lives is to get closer individually to the Savior of the world, and this is also one of the primary reasons that we commemorate Christmas. As the sun is the center of our solar system, so is the Messiah the center of our lives and our families. Without the sun, our solar system would fly apart. Without the Savior's righteousness in our lives and his faith in our hearts, our families and our lives would also fly apart.

Who can think of a more challenging idea than this: that the King of kings is now knocking at our door? He is seeking to bring us the greatest blessings of eternal life. This is also our greatest opportunity that is knocking at our door. For only with his spirit in our hearts can we reach our greatest goals. With his spirit we can also partially reflect his light into some dark corners of our own smaller worlds.

George M. Docherty has pointed out that "the sound of knocking upon a door invariably arouses our immediate interest, and sometimes even a fearful curiosity. In the theater, the audience is held in expectant silence as a heavy hand pounds upon the door upstage. This is also the case when it happens in our homes, especially if one is alone on a winter's evening. Outside a high wind may be howling and hurling cascades of rain against the black window panes. Then suddenly, in a lull of the wind's moaning, a knock is heard at the door."

Even in the uncertain turmoil of our lives, Christ knocks at our bruised and anxious hearts to bring them strength and peace. Of his gift, Mr. Docherty says, "This is a free offer of the gospel of Christ. It comes without money and without price. We should open the doors of our hearts. Rise up from your chairs of ease. Push aside the newspapers and literature of this world that are filling up so much of our lives. Then we should take off the coats of habit that are stifling our outlook. Break away from the routine of spending our days with our cozy, comfortable, contented selves. And by an act of our own free will, go to the doors of our hearts, and throw them open wide that Christ might enter into our lives."

Then when we come to the end of this existence, we may find our eternal home with God. Then may we hear repeated the Charles Dickens' Christmas prayer of Tiny Tim, who said, "God bless us, every one!"

The Music of Christmas

IN A MOST extraordinary statement made in July 1830, the resurrected Jesus instructed the wife of the Prophet Joseph Smith to make a selection of sacred hymns that could be sung in order to help build up the spirits and strengthen the philosophies of his followers. From this magnificent revelation we learn something about how the Master himself feels about great music. He said, "For my soul delighteth in the song of the heart; yea, the song of the righteous is a prayer unto me, and it shall be answered with a blessing upon their heads." (D&C 25:12.)

The scripture gives us many of the great traditions of Christmas that have been increased in power because they have been set to music. We sing songs of praise, worship, and gladness as we recount those events surrounding the birth of the holy Babe in Bethlehem. We also thrill to give musical expression to the Christmas miracles. And we wonder at that vast angelic choir that came all the way from the presence of God to sing their songs of praise and love to him who had been appointed to be the Redeemer of men. Certainly one of the best ways to build up in us the spirit of Christmas, the spirit of righteousness, and the spirit of love is to sing. And it is particularly inspiring to sing those great songs of joy and praise that are characteristic of the Christmas season.

Some of our greatest sources of inspiration are the sacred Christmas anthems, the thrilling Christmas oratorios of praise and worship. We have many inspiring Christmas carols. In one of these we sing "Joy to the World":

> Joy to the world, the Lord will come,
> And earth receive her King!
> Let every heart prepare him room,
> And saints and angels sing.
>
> Rejoice! rejoice! when Jesus reigns,
> And saints their songs employ,
> While fields and floods, rocks, hills, and plains,
> Repeat the sounding joy.

No more will sin and sorrow grow
nor thorns infest the ground;
He'll come and make the blessings flow
Far as the curse was found.

Rejoice! rejoice in the Most High!
While Israel spreads abroad,
Like stars that glitter in the sky,
And ever worship God.

And then we have that other beautiful carol entitled "O Little Town of Bethlehem." The words were written by Phillips Brooks. That wonderful little town of Bethlehem has a great history and there are a number of interesting traditions associated with it. Bethlehem means a place of bread. It was the city of David, the home of Ruth, and the birthplace of the Son of God. Then as we relive that famous night, we sing:

O little town of Bethlehem, How still we see thee lie.
Above thy deep and dreamless sleep The silent stars go by;
Yet in the dark streets shineth The everlasting light.
The hopes and fears of all the years Are met in thee tonight.

For Christ is born of Mary; And gathered all above,
While mortals sleep, the angels keep Their watch of wondering
    love.
O morning stars, together proclaim the holy birth;
And praises sing to God the King, And peace to men on earth.

How silently, how silently, The wondrous gift is given!
So God imparts to human hearts The blessings of his heaven.
No ear may hear his coming; But in this world of sin,
Where meek souls will receive him, still The dear Christ enters in.

One of the greatest of the great carols is "Silent Night." It may be sung around the Christmas fire with the Christmas tree close by. Then with our loved ones all around us we fit these beautiful sentiments to this worshipful melody:

Silent night! Holy night!
All is calm; all is bright
Round yon virgin mother and Child,
Holy infant, so tender and mild.
Sleep in heavenly peace;
Sleep in heavenly peace.

Silent night! Holy night!
Shepherds quake at the sight!
Glories stream from heaven afar;
Heavenly hosts sing Alleluia;
Christ, the Savior, is born!
Christ, the Savior, is born!

Silent night! Holy night!
Son of God, love's pure light
Radiant beams from thy holy face,
With the dawn of redeeming grace,
Jesus, Lord, at thy birth,
Jesus, Lord, at thy birth.

The Lord said that the songs of the righteous are prayers unto him and that they should be answered with blessings upon the heads of those who sing them. We get blessings in so many ways at Christmas. When a great idea passes through our minds it builds up our personality and puts strength into our souls. When harmony and beauty pass through our hearts we become more godlike. They not only help us to become better people, but we also get more and more of the spirit of those things that we sing about.

Sometime ago I read an article about how John MacFarlane composed the great Christmas carol entitled "Far, Far Away on Judea's Plains." In that early pioneer day Mr. MacFarlane was an attorney, a schoolteacher, and a surveyor. In addition to being a musician, he was the leader of the St. George (Utah) choir. He had been asked to write a song to be used in the coming Christmas program. He spent a lot of time trying to create something suitable but to no avail. The right ideas didn't seem to want to come.

On this particular day, he had spent the time in a concerted effort to write some suitable song for Christmas, but he went to bed disappointed and discouraged. How often he had tried and how often he had failed! He had frequently gone to his knees for help, and now in his bed he stared up at the ceiling wishing that he had the inspiration to do what had been asked of him. And while he may not have known it, he had actually been helping to answer his own prayer by storing up great sentiments in his mind, and as he continued his meditations he was preparing this great composition. For a long time he had been depositing in his subconscious mental chambers the hymn's framework, and many of its component parts were now silently falling into place. That night his mind continued its work even after he had fallen into a heavy slumber. Suddenly, in his sleep, he could hear a song that was being put together in that great invention chamber of his mind. And every one of us has been similarly equipped by God with a miraculous receiving center for inspiration.

MacFarlane awakened and quickly started to get out of bed, and as he did so his wife was awakened also. She said to him, "Why are you getting up at this hour, and where you you going?" Her husband said, "I have the song, and I must write it down." She said, "Couldn't you do it just as well in the morning?" He replied, "No, it must be done now."

Dutifully his wife, Ann, also left their bed and followed her husband to the living room. The house was cold, and while he procured his writing materials, humming a song as he did so, his wife revived the banked fire. Both the words and the melody were playing across MacFarlane's mind. As the work of composition continued, he and his wife presented a strange sight. His portly frame, clothed in his nightshirt and stocking cap, was hunched over the organ. His ankles were exposed. At one time his movements would be jerky and hurried, and at another time they would be slow and confident. Beside him was his wife, huddled over his shoulder and clad in her flannel nightclothes. In her stretched-out arms she shifted the lighted candle from one hand to the other in order to give his work the best possible illumination.

Quickly MacFarlane recorded a melodic line and then added the lyrics that had aroused him from his sleep. A selection so new and so dramatic was coming to life that his strong, stirring emotions submerged the world about him and caused him to lose track of time and things. The sporadic squawks and distended chords that came from the house mingled with the cold breezes that were passing through that silent wintry night. In the graying light of the coming dawn, the room grew colder as the banked fire dwindled into a pile of ashes. But the composer could not stop. With one hand he fingered the keyboard, while he wrote his music with the other. From time to time he would lean back and look at his wife, and Ann would smile and nod her approval. Often, at the conclusion of a passage, she would pat his shoulder or squeeze his arm, conveying to him her pride and encouragement. Other hours passed and finally he stood up and stretched himself. As he went to the window the sun was edging the eastern cliffs with pink, gold, and bronze. In the valley the Virgin River picked up the shafts of light so that it glistened like a silver ribbon as it lazily drifted toward the south.

After some contemplation MacFarlane returned to the organ and adjusted himself on the stool. Hesitantly at first, but soon boldly and confidently, he struck the chords. Suddenly the room itself seemed to come to life. His wife picked up the melody and the composer took the strong counter melody of the bass. Together they sang the composition once, twice, and then a third time. At its end, Ann was crying. When the St. George choir sang this song for the first time, it received a wholehearted reception. In the following weeks the people sang it in their homes, in their caroling, and in many other kinds of gatherings. By the following Christmas, people all over the Church were singing the MacFarlane hymn. From the Utah Territory, the song spread across the nation and found itself in Albany and Atlanta, Lafayette and Lincoln. And even across the seas and all around the world, this song was heard. And this was no temporary popularity, for presently in Brussels, Bordeaux, Liverpool and Lausanne, the strains of this great Christmas carol are still pouring forth.

> Far, far away on Judea's plains
> Shepherds of old heard the joyous strains:
> Glory to God, Glory to God,
> Glory to God in the highest;
> Peace on earth, goodwill to men,
> Peace on earth, goodwill to men!
>
> Sweet are these strains of redeeming love,
> Message of mercy from heav'n above:
> Glory to God, Glory to God,
> Glory to God, in the highest;
> Peace on earth, goodwill to men,
> Peace on earth, goodwill to men!
>
> Lord, with the angels we too would rejoice;
> Help us to sing with the heart and voice:
> Glory to God, Glory to God,
> Glory to God in the highest;
> Peace on earth, goodwill to men,
> Peace on earth, goodwill to men!

Hasten the time when, from ev'ry clime,
Men shall unite in these strains sublime:
Glory to God, Glory to God,
Glory to God, in the highest;
Peace on earth, goodwill to men,
Peace on earth, goodwill to men!

And so each Christmas, John MacFarlane's message fills our hearts and rings forth therefrom to tell the people of the world one of the greatest messages of Christmas. And it gives us all a spirit of worship, faith, and joy. And so each year as we sing our inspired music, we lift ourselves up toward God. And may he continue to bless our lives as we attract from him the blessings that he pours out upon our heads because of the songs of our hearts that we sing at Christmas.

Flowers

ONE OF THE great values of our world is its tremendous possession of flowers. I have often pondered about what motivating influences in God's heart caused him to create them. We may be sure that our Heavenly Father is a great lover of beauty, and his floral inventions add much to the harmony, fragrance, and wonder of our own lives. Flowers not only inspire us with their color and fragrance; they also act as symbols of great truths and ambitions. They help us to express our own emotions and happiness, and our righteousness is stimulated by them.

Lydia M. Child said, "How the universal heart of man blesses flowers! They are wreathed round the cradle, the marriage altar and the tomb. They should deck the brow of the youthful bride, for they are in themselves a lovely type of marriage. They should twine round the tomb, for their perpetually renewed beauty is a symbol of the resurrection. They should festoon the altar, for their fragrance and beauty ascend in perpetual worship before the Most High."

Theodore Parker tells us: "Every rose is an autograph from the hand of God to his world about us." He has inscribed his thoughts in these marvelous hieroglyphics which sense and science these many thousands of years have been seeking to understand. Bovee tries to involve us in a marvelous creative process of our own when he says, "To cultivate a garden is to walk with God."

Everyone ought to cultivate several kinds of flower gardens. One of these should be literal, each individual bringing out of God's good earth the most inspirational floral creations of his own choosing. Flowers provide charm for our dinner tables, bringing grace to our rooms and inspiration to our souls. In addition, each of us may plant in his mind a garden of symbols and let the blossoms stand for something even more important than themselves.

For example, what a thrill it is each spring to be motivated by the beautiful, pure white, trumpet-shaped, fragrant lily, the flower of Easter. By its beauty and meaning it helps us to more effectively commemorate the initiation of the universal resurrection upon this earth. The Easter lily is also a symbol of purity, which has a special role in the traditional festival of dawn. With the Easter lily, all nature is reawakened to the anticipation of the enjoyment of a new life.

I once saw many acres of these beautiful Easter lilies, all in a glorious state of full bloom. They seemed like a vast multitude of heavenly angels preaching their own sermons about the resurrection, as though they were all praising God for the immortality of the personality and the eternal glory of the human soul.

After sufficiently contemplating the resurrection, we might change the color and the season to commemorate the birth of the Son of God with the brilliant red Christmas poinsettia. More than almost any other thing, the poinsettia brings into our hearts the unique spirit of the Christmas holidays.

Again we change the spirit to another important holy day called Mother's Day. Our mothers joined in a sacred partnership with God to give us life. And the carnation is the sacred flower breathing its own significance into Mother's Day. We have the brilliant, many-hued peony to help us appropriately commemorate Memorial Day. This is the day set apart to remember the departed. There are several other flowers related to the Memorial Day idea: one is the dainty blue forget-me-not, another is the soldier's poppy. Lieutenant Colonel John McCrae served for four years on the western front in World War I. Just prior to his death on January 28, 1918, he wrote:

> In Flanders fields the poppies blow
> Between the crosses, row on row,
>   That mark our place; and in the sky
>   The larks, still bravely singing, fly
> Scarce heard amid the guns below.
>
> We are the Dead. Short days ago
> We lived, felt dawn, saw sunset glow,
>   Loved and were loved, and now we lie
>   In Flanders fields.

Take up our quarrel with the foe;
To you from failing hands we throw
   The torch; be yours to hold it high.
   If ye break faith with us who die
We shall not sleep, though poppies grow
     In Flanders fields.

A single flower may have great personal significance as it represents individual sentiments. Someone has said:

Take this rose—this tiny rose—
And wear it for a day.
Take the love that with it goes
To keep or throw away.
Just a rosebud kissed by dew,
Kissed by tender teardrops, too,
But it brings my heart to you,
So take this rose.

We have other sentiments connected with flowers. William Wordsworth wrote "The Daffodils."

I wandered lonely as a cloud
   That floats on high o'er vales and hills,
When all at once I saw a crowd,
   A host, of golden daffodils,
Beside the lake, beneath the trees,
Fluttering and dancing in the breeze.

Continuous as the stars that shine
   And twinkle on the Milky Way,
They stretched in never-ending line
   Along the margin of a bay:
Ten thousand saw I at a glance,
Tossing their heads in sprightly dance.

The waves beside them danced, but they
   Outdid the sparkling waves in glee;
A poet could not but be gay
   In such a jocund company.
I gazed, and gazed, but little thought
What wealth the show to me had brought;

For oft, when on my couch I lie
   In vacant or in pensive mood,
They flash upon that inward eye
   Which is the bliss of solitude;
And then my heart with pleasure fills,
And dances with the daffodils.

Robert Loveman changes the mood a little with his stimulating poem entitled "April Rain."

> It isn't raining rain to me,
>   It's raining daffodils;
> In every dimpled drop I see
>   Wild flowers on the hills.
>
> The clouds of gray engulf the day
>   And overwhelm the town;
> It isn't raining rain to me,
>   It's raining roses down.
>
> It isn't raining rain to me,
>   But fields of clover bloom,
> Where any buccaneering bee
>   Can find a bed and room.
>
> A health unto the happy,
>   A fig for him who frets!
> It isn't raining rain to me,
>   It's raining violets.

Flowers not only make our hearts dance; they put twinkles in our eyes and romance in our spirits and cover the entire earth with beauty and fragrance. A great highway running through the city of Winston-Salem, North Carolina, is lined on both sides for many miles with millions of beautiful red climbing roses. They cover the fences and give a lift to all of those who pass along the highway.

For some very good reasons, each state in the union has selected a particular flower to serve as its emblem. The state flower of Kansas is the sunflower. The sunflower is the symbol of loyalty. One of the chief characteristics of the sunflower is that it always follows the sun, not only in the morning when the day is young, but it remains constant and true throughout the long afternoon when the heat is great. As this great orb of the day drops into the sea at evening time, its last admiring glances are received from the ever-loyal sunflower. This helpful symbol can inspire us in perfecting our own loyalties.

The beautiful white flowering dogwood is the state flower of Virginia and North Carolina. There is an ancient tradition that the timber of the cross of Christ was taken from a dogwood tree, and in its sincere humiliation since that time, the dogwood has taken upon itself the marks of the crucifixion. In each of its four-petaled blossoms can still be clearly seen the print of a rusty nail.

The state flower is the sagebrush in Nevada, the orange blossom in Florida, the magnificent rhododendron in Washington, the yucca in New Mexico, and the sego lily in Utah. The bulb of the sego lily did much to keep the early Utah pioneers alive during those long, hard, early starvation years. The most beautiful parts of many plants are the blossoms, but the blossoms also produce the perfume, the color, and the plant's reproductive organs.

Flowers also tell us much about God. Jesus said that a tree should be judged by its fruits, and we can learn about the Creator through his creations. Millions of beautiful flowers tell us that God has a great love of beauty, harmony, and fragrance. He is also very resourceful and knows how to combine inspiration and utility. From these miraculous blossoms we get red apples, yellow peaches, blue plums, purple grapes, green watermelons, and black cherries—all of which are loaded with a variety of life-giving vitamins capable of producing growth, intelligence, vision, love, energy, and greatness in human beings.

The Creator has endowed these creations with the ability to extract from elements in the soil, the water, and the air whatever is necessary for the development of that greatest of all commodities, life. There is an old tradition about a man threatened by starvation who heated up some of the earth's topsoil and ate it with the hope of getting from it the nourishment which he knew it contained. But man is not equipped to use these elements in their natural inorganic form. God's great fruit and vegetable creations, such as the tomato, the apple, the grape, and the potato, have been given the power to transform these elements into an organic form usable by human beings. Therefore, our very lives depend upon our plants with their blossoms.

Certainly it is a great benefit for us to be part of the personal family of such an intelligent, all-wise, and thoughtful Creator, and we also become heirs of all the benefits of his resourcefulness. God didn't actually put his greatest beauty, utility, or wonder into his flowers. He put his greatest gifts into his own children. God hid up his treasures of gold, oil, and diamonds in the earth, but he endowed his children with his own attributes and potentials.

What about developing our own gardens with beautiul flowers of faith, virtue, love, generosity, kindness, fairness, and a love of righteousness? Jesus was very familiar with the miracles of agriculture, horticulture, and flower culture. He talked about the sower, the husbandman, the vinedresser, and the lilies of the field. However, he used these expressions primarily to point out even greater truths for our benefit. Jesus was not primarily concerned with producing better wheat crops or higher fruit yields. He always had in mind the production of better human beings. He was speaking of people when he mentioned eliminating the vine's wild branches and pruning out the tree's dead wood and doing away with those useless limbs that were unproductive. We know that he wants us to build greater beauty, color, harmony, and utility into ourselves.

One may be able to live without fragrance, beauty, and inspiration, but not very well. Many hundreds of years ago an old Persian philosopher said:

> If of thy mortal goods thou art bereft,
> And from thy slender store two loaves
>   to thee are left,
> Sell one, and with the dole
> Buy hyacinths to feed thy soul.
>
> —Gulistan of Moslih Eddin Saadi

Someone has said that if you are in a strange city without friends, food, or resources and have only fifty cents to your name, take your money and get a shoeshine. Above most other things we need to maintain the inspiration of our own lives. On a plaque placed on an old garden wall in England is written this inscription:

> Men go to their gardens for pleasure;
> Go, thou, to thy garden for prayer;
> The Lord walks in the cool of the evening
> With those who seek sanctity there.

What a thrill it must have been in that early morning of the Creation when God planted a garden eastward in Eden! He must have had great joy as he walked in its refreshing environment. I am confident that in God's eternal heaven, he has beautiful gardens producing flowers and fragrance and fruit and happiness. Helen Keller was blind, deaf, and dumb so far as her physical senses were concerned, but she inspires us with her poem "In the Garden of the Lord," in which she says:

And my blind eyes were touched with light,
And there was laid upon my lips a flame of fire.

May God bless us that our blind eyes may learn to see and that our lips may learn to speak so that we will be able to appreciate, praise, and utilize the blessings that he has provided for our use, and may he help us to be good gardeners.

Christis in America

THE LAST MONTH of the year, especially December 25, is set aside to commemorate the birth of the Savior of the world. The coming of Christ is undoubtedly the most important event that has ever taken place upon our earth. The details of his life, birth, and death were known in advance in many lands. One of the most important parts of the earth then and now is what is known as the western hemisphere. Here the Creator placed some of the earth's richest soil and most beautiful scenery, and some of its richest metal and oil reserves. Some of God's most favored children have lived upon this continent, both before and after Columbus. The news of the birth, death, and mission of Jesus was also known upon this continent.

For a long period, both before and after his birth, a high state of culture existed here that was probably the equal of any in the East. The ancestors of the Indians have left evidence in their hieroglyphics and legends that a great white god once visited them. It said that he came down from heaven and after teaching them the gospel and establishing his church among them, he returned to heaven. We received an authentic explanation of this tradition when, in 1829, in upper New York state, a great volume of pre-Columbus scripture was made known to us, written on metallic plates in a language called reformed Egyptian.

These records had lain hidden since the once-righteous part of the inhabitants of this land had been destroyed in a devastating war that had wiped out their civilization. This pre-Columbus volume of scripture was translated under the inspiration of God, by a young American prophet named Joseph Smith, into a record known as the Book of Mormon. On at least two different occasions the Lord tried to build up a great nation upon this continent. Each time the people have done well for a time, but have then turned away and have been destroyed as have been so many other civilizations of the past.

The Indians that were living here when Columbus arrived were descendants of a colony of Israelites that had been led away from Jerusalem six hundred years before Christ. They brought with them many of the Old Testament scriptures. To these were added the writings of their own prophets. Five years before Christ's birth in Bethlehem, a prophet known as Samuel the Lamanite came among the people to warn them of their wickedness. He also foretold the birth of Jesus in Bethlehem. Among other things, he told the people that at the time of his birth a sign should be given—there would be a day and a night and another day in which there would be no darkness. (Helaman 14:2-6.) On that first American Christmas the sun went down as usual but, because of great lights in the heavens, there was no darkness.

Many unusual things happened on both continents at the time of Jesus' birth as well as at the time of his death. In the eastern hemisphere they had the Bethlehem star, and Gabriel and other heavenly angels took part in a great program. At the crucifixion there was darkness over all the land from the sixth to the ninth hour. (Matthew 27:44.) Matthew also says:

"And, behold, the veil of the temple was rent in twain from the top to the bottom; and the earth did quake, and the rocks rent;

"And the graves were opened; and many bodies of the saints which slept arose,

"And came out of the graves after his resurrection, and went into the holy city, and appeared unto many." (Matthew 27:51-53.)

About some of the signs which were to be given in the West, the prophet Samuel said:

"But behold, . . . in that day that he shall suffer death the sun shall be darkened and refuse to give his light unto you; and also the moon and the stars; and there shall be no light upon the face of this land, even from the time that he shall suffer death, for the space of three days, to the time that he shall rise again from the dead.

"And many graves shall be opened, and shall yield up many of their dead; and many saints shall appear unto many.

"And behold, thus hath the angel spoken unto me; for he said unto me that there should be thunderings and lightnings for the space of many hours." (Helaman 14:20, 25-26.)

Among the most valuable possessions of our world are the four Gospels. These are four inspired New Testament histories that tell of the life and teachings of Jesus. They were written for the specific purpose of spreading Christ's message of salvation. The first three Gospels are called the Synoptic Gospels. They give a synopsis of Christ's teachings, make a general presentation, and were written some thirty years after the resurrection.

Each of the Gospel authors had a different purpose in writing. Matthew wrote the first Gospel for the benefit of his Jewish countrymen. Mark wrote the second Gospel primarily for the Romans. Luke was in Greece when he wrote the third Gospel for the benefit of the Greeks. Many years later John wrote the fourth Gospel to help the Christians and to provide some training in faith for those who had entered into the new kingdom of Christ.

However, all four Gospels together fall far short of exhausting the possible gospel subject matter. If all of the words spoken by Jesus, as recorded in these four Gospels, were put together into one account, they could be read in about thirty minutes. In concluding his gospel, John says:

"And there are also many other things which Jesus did, the which, if they should be written every one, I suppose that even the world itself could not contain the books that should be written." (John 21:25.)

Now we have a fifth gospel. This is an instructive record of Christ's post-resurrection visit to the western continent, written by a pre-Columbus American prophet named Nephi. It gives a magnificent account of the visit of the Savior upon the western continent.

Jesus knew about heaven and hell. He knew about the last days. Certainly he knew about America. He also knows about our present-day problems and is very anxious that we solve them properly. This very interesting and important American gospel can be very helpful. It provides us with a thrilling, additional, and independent witness of the divinity of Jesus Christ. It lets us know in a very special way that Jesus Christ is the God of this land. It was no accident that the center of Christian gravity is now in America. It gives us many other gospel truths that would not otherwise be known.

When Jesus appeared in ancient America, the people to whom he came were gathered around their temple in the Land Bountiful. They were surveying the damage and talking about the terrible destruction that had so recently taken place in consequence of their disobedience. While they were conversing, they heard a voice as if it came out of heaven. They cast their eyes round about, for they understood not what the voice said. It was not a loud voice, neither was it a harsh voice, and not-withstanding it was a small voice, it seemed to pierce them to the center and caused them to quake. (3 Nephi 11:3.)

The voice came a second time and they heard it, but again they understood it not. The third time the voice came, they opened their ears and their eyes were toward the sound thereof; and as they looked steadfastly toward heaven, they heard the voice say unto them, "Behold my Beloved Son, in whom I am well pleased, in whom I have glorified my name—hear ye him." (3 Nephi 11:7.) They saw a man clothed in a white robe coming down out of heaven, and he descended until he stood in their midst. Then the resurrected Jesus introduced himself and recounted the experiences of his life and death.

He invited them to inspect the nail prints in his hands and the sword wound in his side. Then he taught them the principles of the gospel as he had done among the people of the East. As he taught them, he gave them specific instructions to write down the things he had said. Thus we have the "fifth Gospel," which in point of time of writing was actually the first one written. It also has the distinction of being directly and specifically authorized by the Lord himself and written at the very time that the events took place. (3 Nephi 16:4.)

Now, as we commemorate the birth of Christ more than 1970 years after the original Christmas, both of our continents are in serious trouble because we too have disobeyed his teach-ings. More than ever before, the greatest message there is for our world is the Christmas message. It is the message that God lives, that Jesus Christ is the Savior of all mankind, and that if we obey him we may sometime become like him.

It is wonderful each year to go across the seas for Christmas. Bethlehem will always be the honored birthplace of the Son of God. But God is also the God of America. He has made us several visits. He desires to bless our land. America has a great past and a brilliant future. May we so live that he will feel that America is a land where he is highly honored. And may God help us that as we follow him we may be the kind of Christians that would greatly please him.

Christmas and Christ's Second Coming

ACCORDING TO THE divine plan, our earth has been allotted a mortal existence of seven thousand years, which was patterned after the seven days of the creation. In six days the Lord created the heavens and the earth and all that in them is, and he rested the seventh day. The Lord designated the seventh day as the Sabbath, and he blessed the Sabbath day and hallowed it. Following this pattern, we have been given six thousand years in which to do the work of our planet, and during the seventh one thousand years the earth will rest from its wickedness and we will enjoy the earth's millennium, which will be the most blessed and happy period that has ever been known upon our earth up to this time.

This earth is now a telestial sphere, but during the millennium its status will be increased to that of a terrestrial earth. That is, its paradisiacal glory will be restored and it will be like it was in the Garden of Eden before the fall. Then, after the thousand years of the millenium and after all of the unfinished business of our world has been taken care of, the earth will again have its status increased. This time it will be given its celestial glory, and those who have become celestial people will inhabit it forever and forever.

During the earth's seventh one-thousand years, Christ will reign personally upon the earth, and both mortal and immortal beings will abide here. This will be the condition that will most expeditiously prepare our earth and its prospective permanent residents for the wonderful destiny of a celestial planet inhabited by celestial beings. The celestial kingdom is made up of that highest order of life of which God himself is a member. The purpose of the gospel is to get us into the celestial kingdom. And in our journey toward that end we have certain things that must be accomplished.

We have had some very important milestones making up our earth's history. During the first one-thousand-year period people lived a very long time and had some important combinations of good and bad. Cain started the first crime wave by killing his

brother Abel. In the second one-thousand years one group became so righteous that the city of Enoch and all of its people
were translated and taken up into heaven in the year of the
world 1052. And by the year 1663 the people had become so
wicked that the great flood of waters was sent to destroy the
people. After the flood the Lord started our earth's civilization
over again, beginning with Noah and his family.

Some 345 years after the flood and approximately 2,008
years after the birth of Adam and about 1996 years B.C., a great
giant of faith was born upon the earth by the name of Abraham.
God wanted to make of Abraham's posterity the greatest nation
that had ever been known upon the earth. And in the year of the
world 2433, some 1571 years B.C., God came down onto the top of
Mount Sinai in a cloud of fire and gave that great code of laws
centered in the Ten Commandments.

Solomon became the king of Israel in the year of the world
2989, or 1015 B.C. He was blessed with greater wisdom than anyone who had ever lived upon the earth. But later in his life he
turned away from God and did some very foolish things. In direct
violation of the word of the Lord he married some idolatrous
women, and as the Lord had foretold, they led Solomon himself
into idolatry. When Solomon died, he was very much out of
favor with God. After his death, Rehoboam, the son of Solomon
and an idol-worshiping wife, succeeded his father upon the
throne of Israel. And as a result of wickedness, the Israelite
nation was rejected by God. If Solomon had provided Rehoboam
with a Jehovah-worshiping mother, the history of Israel may
have been quite different. Later, the kingdom was divided, and
ten of the twelve tribes were led away into captivity, and God's
great objectives for a righteous people were scuttled and fell by
the wayside. Therefore, God's hopes for a righteous people had
again failed as it had done so many times both before and since.

It is probable that the two most important events that ever
have taken place or ever will take place upon this earth are
centered in the visits that the Son of God has made and will make
to it. At Christmas time we recount his birth in Bethlehem. According to our best chronology, Jesus was born about 4004 years
after the birth of Adam, which was about 2340 years after the
earth had been devastated and cleansed by the flood.

When Jesus was thirty years of age, he began his public ministry, and in the following three years he established his church upon the earth and taught the doctrines of salvation. He finally gave his own life upon the cross as a part of the program of redeeming us from death. He also initiated the universal resurrection.

Since the time of his birth in Bethlehem, another 1973 years have passed, which now brings us up to the approximate year of the world 5977. If this chronology is correct, twenty-three more years will bring us to the year of the world 6000. This will be the time set for the events scheduled to come at the end of the six thousand years and the beginning of the seventh. This is the general time appointed for the second coming of Christ and the beginning of the millennium.

Of course, no one knows exactly when the second coming of Christ will take place. This is the Lord's own secret, and he has said that not even the angels in heaven know the day nor the hour nor will they know until the event takes place. However, we do know that his time schedule is running out, and the signs all indicate that his coming is near.

Just before his crucifixion, while he was foretelling his own glorious second coming to the earth, he pointed out that his church should previously be officially restored to the earth and he said: "And this gospel of the kingdom shall be preached in all the world as a witness unto all nations, and then shall the end come." The star of Bethlehem announced his coming to the wise men in the East. The angel Gabriel and a large company of angels appeared to the shepherds tending their flocks upon the Judean hills and created some very pleasant situations. He has also described the wars and wickedness that would precede his second coming.

Even while living in Palestine nearly twenty centuries ago, Jesus was keenly aware of us who live now and the problems that presently beset us. And under the very shadow of the cross, he looked down to our time and made a rather uncomplimentary comparison when he said: ". . . as the days of Noe were, so also shall the coming of the Son of man be." (Matthew 24:37.) He gave us a sign when he said: "Now learn a parable of the fig tree; When his branch is yet tender, and putteth forth leaves, ye know that summer is nigh: So likewise ye, when ye shall see all these things, know that it is near, even at the doors." (Matthew 24:32-33.)

As important as it is for us to look back over the last 1900 years and commemorate the events surrounding his birth, life, and death, it may be even more important for us to look ahead a few years in anticipation of his glorious return visit to the earth to cleanse it and us of sin and to inaugurate his glorious millennial reign. We have several reasons to expect that there may be many people presently living upon the earth who will have a personal part to play in his second coming.

The Bible accurately predicted Christ's first coming in all details hundreds of years before they took place. It was made known that he would come from the tribe of Judah, that his birthplace would be in Bethlehem, that he would be born of a virgin, that he would flee into Egypt, that he would heal the sick, that he would be rejected, betrayed, and sold for thirty pieces of silver, that he would take upon himself the sins of the world and be crucified with sinners, that his side would be pierced, and that he should be the first fruits of the resurrection. It was also foretold that he would rise from the dead on the third day.

However, it is very interesting that the same prophets recorded in the same Bible many of the details of his second coming. They have all pointed out that his second coming should be in a very different manner. The first time he came as a man of sorrows and acquainted with grief. The second time he will come as the Almighty God. He came the first time as the Prince of Peace. He will come the second time as the King of kings and Lord of lords. He came the first time to atone for our sins by his own suffering on condition of our repentance and obedience. When he comes the second time to judge the sinners who have not repented, it will be our turn to do some suffering. And it might be very profitable for us, while we are commemorating his first coming, to give some consideration to some of those prophecies that foretell his second coming. The apostle Paul said, "The Lord Jesus shall be revealed from heaven with his mighty angels in flaming fire, taking vengeance on those who know not God and that obey not the gospel of the Lord Jesus Christ."

Jude said: "And Enoch also, the seventh from Adam, prophesied of these, saying, Behold, the Lord cometh with ten thousands of his saints, To execute judgment upon all, and to convince all that are ungodly among them of all their ungodly deeds which they have ungodly committed, and of all their hard speeches which ungodly sinners have spoken against him." (Jude 14:15.)

The psalmist said, "Our God shall come, and shall not keep silence: a fire shall devour before him, and it shall be very tempestuous round about him. He shall call to the heavens from above, and to the earth, that he may judge his people. Gather my saints together unto me; those that have made a covenant with me by sacrifice." (Psalm 50:3-5.)

The prophet Joel said: "The sun and the moon shall be darkened, and the stars shall withdraw their shining. The Lord also shall roar out of Zion, and utter his voice from Jerusalem; and the heavens and the earth shall shake: but the Lord will be the hope of his people, and the strength of the children of Israel. So shall ye know that I am the Lord your God dwelling in Zion, my holy mountain: then shall Jerusalem be holy, and there shall no strangers pass through her any more." (Joel 3:15-17.)

Through Malachi, God said: "Behold, I will send my messenger, and he shall prepare the way before me: and the Lord, whom ye seek, shall suddenly come to his temple, even the messenger of the covenant, whom ye delight in: behold, he shall come, saith the Lord of hosts. But who may abide the day of his coming? and who shall stand when he appeareth? . . ." (Malachi 3:1-2.) And we might say, "Who indeed?" Then Jesus himself said to his disciples, "For the Son of man shall come in the glory of his Father with his angels; and then he shall reward every man according to his works." (Matthew 16:27.)

And Paul, speaking to the Thessalonian saints, said, "But I would not have you to be ignorant, brethren, concerning them which are asleep, that ye sorrow not, even as others which have no hope. For if we believe that Jesus died and rose again, even so them also which sleep in Jesus will God bring with him. For this we say unto you by the word of the Lord, that we which are alive and remain unto the coming of the Lord shall not prevent them which are asleep. For the Lord himself shall descend from heaven with a shout, with the voice of the archangel, and with the trump of God: and the dead in Christ shall rise first: Then we which are alive and remain shall be caught up together with them in the clouds, to meet the Lord in the air: and so shall we ever be with the Lord." (1 Thessalonians 4:13-17.)

I remember the old days out on the farm when the six days of labor were spent in getting ready for the Sabbath day. Saturday was the time when all of our possible chores were done, which would enable us to properly keep the Sabbath, and the Sabbath was a different kind of day from the other six. And Saturday night was the time set apart to clean up ourselves. This was when we had the traditional Saturday night bath. This was when we laid out our Sunday clothing and made all other possible preparations for this very special day.

Our earth is now just about to get its Saturday night bath. And what a bath it will be! And some of us who objected to having our ears scrubbed in the old days had better be prepared, for we may be sure that the scrubbing that our earth will get will really be something. And it will not be very pleasant for those who have not obeyed the message given during his first coming.

John the Revelator looked forward to his actual coming and said: "Behold, he cometh with clouds; and every eye shall see him, and they also which pierced him: and all kindreds of the earth shall wail because of him." (Revelation 1:7.)

While it is wonderful for us to keep Christmas by looking back to his peaceful pleasant birth in Bethlehem, it might be much more profitable for us now to also keep Christmas by living the lessons of his life and looking forward to that much more exciting day when he will come again. And if we properly clean up our own lives now, it may not be necessary for us to undergo the other cleansing that has been described.

Christmas in August

SOMETIME AGO I heard a great mother give an account of the happy Christmas period that had just been enjoyed by the members of her family. They had had a time of interesting festivities, entertainments, and dinners. Their Christmas decorations had been especially beautiful. The family members had become much closer to each other as they had sung Christmas carols around the Christmas fire. There had been a fine feeling of fellowship, helpfulness, and good will grow up among family members. Presents had been exchanged. All of this had been capped by a sincere spirit of worship and thanksgiving to God for their many blessings.

During this season there had been a complete absence of any bickering or any other signs of ill will in the household. The youngest daughter had been so impressed with the elevated attitudes and happiness that Christmas had given to her family that she had said, "Mommy, why can't we have Christmas all of the time?" And that is a great idea and one that, if followed, could be extremely profitable.

Actually, Christmas is not just a time to think about the birth of Christ. It is even more important that we learn to think about and appreciate what he did later on, not only in his life, but also in his death and resurrection. These later events are the things that gave his birth much of its significance. And the greatest of substance was also given to our own objectives when Jesus gave us that famous two-word success formula in which he said, "Follow me."

As this interesting mother thoughtfully recounted the story of her family's Christmas commemoration, I thought about a story that I once heard that came out of World War I. A young married man had been taken into military service, and after his training was completed he was sent to fight on the battlefields of France. During his long absence from home, some problems had developed by which his wife was finally led into a very serious moral transgression. The great shock that she received from her unplanned sin made her feel terrible. Accordingly she spent a lot of time in contemplation of what she had done and what she wanted out of life. In her unhappy situation, she tried to understand those influences that had brought this unpleasant circumstance about.

More than anything else she wanted to make sure that such a thing would never happen again, and she planned to make certain that no weakness was allowed to remain in her life that could cause her any future trouble in this or any other of life's problem areas. And she decided that to make her repentance complete and give her the peace of mind that she so desperately wanted, she would sit down and write her husband a letter telling him what had happened and how she felt about it. She told him of the resolutions she had made about the future. Then she asked for his forgiveness and told him of her great love for him and her determination to so live that she could make up for her mistake in every possible way, both to herself and to him. She planned on devoting her life to making him happy.

Her letter was sent but it was not delivered to him at the time expected because his company had been transferred. And because of the secrecy surrounding troop movements there were long delays, and for the next few months her letter was reforwarded several times as it followed her husband about Europe, going as it did from one transfer location to another. Then finally he was released and came home without having received his wife's letter. He was delighted to be home again. He thought that his wife was a wonderful person and he loved her very much.

She, of course, expected that he would bring up the matter mentioned in her letter. And over a few weeks she wondered why he did not do so, but he seemed so happy to be home and she was so pleased to have him that she decided to let him bring it up when he got around to it. And so both went on as if nothing had happened. And it was not until several weeks after he had returned home that the letter was finally delivered to him. It came one day while his wife was out shopping. He read the letter carefully and thoughtfully. He had a great feeling of gratitude that the problem no longer existed. Then he got down on his knees and thanked the Lord for the great character qualities that his wife had exhibited in her handling of this very serious situation. He decided that such a wife was worthy of his greatest love and confidence, and he promised the Lord that he would follow his wife's example by making an exhaustive introspection of his own life and then drawing some plans for the improvement of his own situation.

He also expressed his appreciation to the Lord for the great principles of righteousness given in the gospel on which all human happiness depends and by which all lives should be guided. During the previous Christmas when part of the world had been commemorating the birth of Jesus in Bethlehem and retelling the stories of the wise men following the Bethlehem star to the stable in order to lay their presents at the feet of their newborn king, he had been engaged in the rude and unpleasant business of conquering a dangerous enemy. And he remembered that, with his concern for winning the war, he had not thought very much about Christmas or Christmas presents for anyone, even for his wife. And inasmuch as his wife's shopping would not be completed for about another hour, he decided that he would do some shopping on his own. And inasmuch as it was now August, he should not put off any longer the pleasure of getting his wife a Christmas present.

He left her a note where she would see it when she returned home. He told her that he had gone to get her Christmas present, which he did not send to her last December, and that they were going to have their Christmas now even though it was August. He also told her to be ready, as he would be back in time to take her out to dinner. In addition, he wanted to express his love for her and get her approval about some of the other details for their August Christmas celebration.

James M. Barric once said that God gave us memories that we might have roses in December. And God gave us character qualities and a desire to be obedient that we might commemorate his birthday not only in August but in every other month of the year. Actually, there isn't anything wrong in commemorating Christmas every day. The day of Christ's birth was not the only important day of his life. Every day that he lived was an important day. And Jesus made known the purpose of his own total mission by saying, "I am come that they might have life, and that they have it more abundantly." (John 10:10.)

And to help us to do our part of increasing our life's abundance, he gave us the great gospel laws. In the first two of these he said, "Thou shalt love the Lord thy God with all thy heart, and with all thy soul, and with all thy mind. This is the first and the great commandment and the second is like unto it, Thou shalt love thy neighbour as thyself. On these two commandments hang all the law and the prophets." (Matthew 22:37-40.)

We have been given a lot of other laws as well as some organized institutions to help us make our own lives successful and happy. Governments were instituted by God for the benefit of man, and he will hold us responsible for our acts in relation to them. He himself established this nation by raising up wise men to write our national constitution and establish our government upon Christian principles. He gave us such men as our founding fathers to stand in the forefront of our civilization and give our nation its start toward its destiny. God also established another great institution when he ordained that each of us might belong to his own family. Even before this earth was created, God organized the family unit in heaven to be the basis of our happiness, our success, our education, and our eternal welfare.

He said: "It is not good that man should be alone." And he might have said, "It is not good for woman to be alone, and it is not good for children to be alone." Men, women, and children were created to live together and to love each other and to serve each other. Then, in addition, God gave us this great organization of the Church with its life-producing and life-giving principles and doctrines. One of the first and most important principles of the gospel is the principle of repentance. By the use of this great idea we can cleanse ourselves of evil and then forever exclude from our lives all that is low or detrimental or unworthy by turning our courses upward to more worthwhile things.

God has also given us another great principle, called faith, whereby we can attach ourselves to the greatest philosophies and finest success principles that even God himself can devise. There are many reasons why we commemorate the birth of the Son of God in Bethlehem, and one is that he spent his life in teaching us righteousness and then he himself served as our example. God the Father as well as his Son both live by these great principles that they have tried so hard to get us to adopt. And our Savior and Redeemer is also our greatest example of willingness to forgive. He even prayed for his enemies as they were crucifying him. Out of the pain and anguish caused by his suffering on the cross, he said: "Father, forgive them; for they know not what they do." (Luke 23:34.) This is also an example for us. And he has said that we should forgive those who trespass against us, not only seven times but seventy times seven.

Certainly one of the magnificent Christmas thoughts of Jesus was that we should love our families and build them up and make them strong, happy, and successful. The Lord wants us to be effective in our occupations and constructive in all of our social relationships. But he made our wives and families our primary concern and the place of our greatest opportunities. And President David O. McKay once said that no other success could ever compensate for failure in the home. It helps us to understand this idea when we think of what Jesus meant when he went far enough down the list to say that we should even love our enemies and that we should pray for those who despitefully use us and persecute us. He taught that the philosophy of retaliation is a doctrine of evil and that the practice of requiring an eye for an eye ends eventually in making everybody blind.

Jesus gave his own philosophy of life in the Golden Rule, and someone wrote about a great Christmas attitude when he said, "I will not let my enemy make me sin." That is, I will not give anger for anger or hate for hate. If my friend or my enemy makes a mistake or sins against me, I will not hold it over his head nor try to beat him down and destroy his pride and happiness by constantly reminding him of his error. Neither will I make the same mistake myself, but I will always do unto others as I would have them do unto me. Even our forgiveness of other people does not need to be announced with a trumpet so as to embarrass them. But when we have great love in our hearts, it heals all wounds and give us great power to lift other people up to God and righteousness and success.

And what a tremendous opportunity we have within the walls of our own homes to help people. Have you ever seen someone who was brokenhearted? Or have you ever seen your daughter or your wife or your mother cry and sob as though she could never be comforted? There are many ways that we can win God's approval. However, when I go to stand before the judgment, I can think of very few compliments that I would rather receive from God than for his assurance that I had made my wife happy, my parents proud, and my children faithful.

And I am particularly inspired by this great idea of this returned army veteran who celebrated Christmas in August. One of the finest Christmas ideas with which I am familiar is that by following the example and living the principles of Jesus, we can greatly build other people up and actually commemorate Christmas every day of the year. May God bless us that it may be so, so that we may have Christmas in August and happiness throughout our lives.

The Vision of Sir Launfal

IN 1848 JAMES RUSSELL LOWELL published a great narrative poem entitled "The Vision of Sir Launfal." The poem has to do with the search made for the Holy Grail by one of the knights of King Arthur's court. Sir Launfal was one of the noblemen of the realm who had large possessions and great power. He lived in a magnificent castle and entertained many of the famous lords and ladies of England.

According to an ancient legend, the Holy Grail was the cup out of which Jesus drank during the Last Supper when he met with his disciples in the upper room. The story has it that after his resurrection, this cup was taken to England by Joseph of Arimathea. There it remained for many years in the custody of Joseph's descendants, where it became the object of many pilgrimages and much adoration.

However, it was incumbent upon the custodians of the Holy Grail to keep themselves chaste in thought, word, and deed, and always live above any possible reproach. And because one of the keepers failed in this important requirement, the Holy Grail disappeared. Then many of the greatest knights of King Arthur's round table went in search of it in order to bring its blessings back to the people. Inasmuch as it could not be retained by anyone with an impure life, it naturally followed that it would be the greatest personal honor to the one who was able to recover it.

Finally the great Sir Launfal himself decided to take up the search. And he made a vow that he would never again sleep in a bed or allow the comforts of a pillow under his head until he should begin to keep his vow, nor would he ever stop searching for the Holy Grail until it was found. Then as he lay on a bed of rushes prior to beginning his quest, he had a dream in which he spent his entire lifetime in this important undertaking. In his dream he lived through all of the wanderings, privations, and sufferings that would naturally be connected with such a search. But because of the devotion and service given by this proud knight, his character and personality were changed and rebuilt in such a way that he was fitted to effectively reflect the spirit of the lowly Nazarene himself. When Sir Launfal awoke the next morning resolved to spend the rest of his days living the lessons that he had learned in the experiences of his God given vision.

There are also a great many lessons that we can transfer to ourselves from this delightful poem. Frequently one may feel a thing so strongly and deeply that mere prose may make its expression inadequate. Words can sometimes be made stronger by adding music, meter, harmony, rhyme, and the power of a more forceful expression. On these occasions we may leave the lower regions of communication and rise to that more elegant form of speech that has been measured, weighed, powerized, and set to music. This kind of poem cannot be skimmed over as one might do in reading a newspaper story. Poetry must be read slowly with alert attention given to the pictures that are presented in every line.

The ideas of this great poem are so constructed that they dissolve in one's mind. Each paragraph gives up its own particular thought to the reader. Every human being has a kind of poetic instinct. Each of us has been touched with a hunger for beauty and a craving for music in our speech. And everyone with this genuine poetic instinct loves the rhythm of the verse no less than the thought it contains. It is good for one's soul occasionally to climb to some mountaintop of thought and reverently spend a few hours in this magic land of poetic beauty. We can get ideas from prose, but poetry gives us the spirit in which the ideas are dressed. The poem also sets the mood that the ideas exemplify. It prepares a seedbed in the heart and creates a climate in which the ideas may grow most effectively. Poetry is like a lecture that has enough visual aids and sound effects to dissolve the great ideals and make them available to the bloodstream.

This poem begins by giving us a picture of the landscape that embodies the emotional spirit of the poem, before the story itself is set before us. Lowell draws us a technicolor picture of that great doctrine of Jesus, which says, "Inasmuch as ye have done it unto one of the least of these my brethren, ye have done it unto me." (Matthew 25:40.) But poetry not only gives us its teaching, it also brings on an awakening in us. It furnishes the arousing that gives the ideas their power. The warm, stirring, religious impulses in this poem incite our spirits by translating theological truths into their more noble action form.

In a great poem our own imagination can learn to fly with a freer wing, develop a greater enthusiasm, and experience a more genuine enjoyment. We now go with Sir Launfal on the divine mission embodied in his own life, as he leaves the security and abundance of his own great castle in search of the Holy Grail. As the vision begins to dawn we hear him say:

> My golden spurs now bring to me,
> And bring to me my richest mail,
> For tomorrow I go over land and sea
> In search of the Holy Grail. . . .
>
> The drawbridge dropped with a surly clang,
> And through the dark arch a charger sprang,
> Bearing Sir Launfal, the maiden knight,
> In his gilded mail, that flamed so bright
> It seemed the dark castle had gathered all
> Those shafts that the fierce sun had shot over its wall
> In his siege of three hundred summers long,
> And, binding them all in one blazing sheaf,
> Had cast them forth, so young and strong,
> And lightsome as a locust-leaf.
> Sir Launfal flashed forth in his unscarred mail,
> To seek in all climes for the Holy Grail.

It was morning in the sky and it was morning in the young knight's life as his quest began. As he cleared the drawbridge,

> He was 'ware of a leper, crouched by the gate,
> Who begged with his hand and moaned as he sate;
> And a loathing over Sir Launfal came.
> The sunshine went out of his soul with a thrill,
> The flesh 'neath his armor did shrink and crawl,
> And midway in its leap, his heart stood still
>
> Like a frozen waterfall;
> For this man, so foul and bent of stature,
> Rasped harshly against his dainty nature,
> And seemed the one blot on the summer morn—
> So he tossed him a piece of gold in scorn.
>
> But the leper raised not the gold from the dust:
> "Better to me the poor man's crust,

> Better the blessing of the poor,
> Though I turn me empty from his door,
> That is no true alms which the hand can hold;
> He gives only the worthless gold
> Who gives from a sense of duty;
> But he who gives but a slender mite,
> And gives of that which is out of sight,
> That thread of the all-sustaining Beauty
> Which runs through all and doth all unite—
> The hand cannot clasp the whole of his alms,
> The heart outstretches its eager palms,
> For a God goes with it and makes it store
> To the soul that was starving in darkness before."

Then for all of the long life which was spent in his dream, Sir Launfal searched for his treasure without success, and after many years he returned armorless, horseless, penniless, and old to the castle that had once been his home. It is now the opposite time of year from the season when his quest began. It is also the opposite time of his life. The air is filled with cold and ice. It is the middle of winter, and it is the Christmastime. Sir Launfal's hair is now thin and gray, his clothing is worn and comfortless. Mr. Lowell says:

> But the wind without was eager and sharp;
> Of Sir Launfal's gray hair it makes a harp,
> And rattles and wrings the icy strings,
> Singing in dreary monotone,
> A Christmas carol of its own,
> Whose burden still, as he might guess,
> Was "shelterless, shelterless, shelterless!"
>
> The voice of the seneschal flared like a torch
> As he shouted the wanderer away from the porch,
> And he sat in the gateway and saw all night
> The great hall-fire so cheery and bold
> Through the window-slits of the castle old.
> Built out of its piers of ruddy light
> Against the drift of the cold.
>
> There was never a leaf on bush or tree,
> The bare boughs rattled shudderingly;
> The river was dumb and could not speak,
> For the weaver Winter its shroud had spun;
> A single crow in the treetop bleak
> From his shining feathers shed off the cold sun;

Again it was morning, but shrunk and cold
As if her veins were sapless and old,
And she rose up decrepitly
For a last dim look at the earth and sea.

Sir Launfal turned from his own hard gate,
For another heir in his earldom sate;
An old, bent man, worn out and frail,
He came back from seeking the Holy Grail.
Little he recked of his earldom's loss;
No more on his surcoat was blazoned the cross;
But deep in his soul the sign he wore,
The badge of the suffering and the poor.

Sir Launfal's raiment thin and spare
Was idle mail 'gainst the barbed air,
For it was just at the Christmas time,
So he mused, as he sat, of a sunnier clime,
And sought for some shelter from cold and snow
In the light and warmth of long ago;

Then Sir Launfal was again made aware of the pitiful beggar
at his side, suffering from hunger, disease, and cold. The beggar's
flesh was white with leprosy, and he said to Sir Launfal, "For
Christ's sweet sake, I beg an alms." But Sir Launfal saw this gruesome human being with a different emotion than that which had
been excited in him on this very spot so many years before. In the
gruesome sight Sir Launfal saw:

The leper, lank as the rain-blanched bone,
That cowers beside him, a thing as lone
And white as the ice-isles of Northern seas
In the desolate horror of his disease.

And Sir Launfal said, "I behold in thee
An image of Him who died on the tree.
Thou also hast had thy crown of thorns;
Thou also hast had the world's buffets and scorns;
And to thy life were not denied
The wounds in the hands and feet and side.
Mild Mary's Son, acknowledge me;
Behold through him, I give to thee."
Then the soul of the leper stood up in his eyes
And looked at Sir Launfal, and straightway he
Remembered in what a haughtier guise
He had flung an alms to leprosy,

When he girt his young life up in gilded mail
And set forth in search of the Holy Grail.

The heart within him was ashes and dust;
He parted in twain his single crust,
He broke the ice on the streamlet's brink,
And gave the leper to eat and drink;

'Twas a mouldy crust of coarse brown bread,
'Twas water out of a wooden bowl—
Yet with fine wheaten bread was the leper fed,
And 'twas red wine he drank with his thirsty soul.

As Sir Launfal mused with a downcast face,
A light shone round about the place;
The leper no longer crouched at his side,
But stood before him glorified,
Shining and tall and fair and straight
As the pillar that stood by the Beautiful Gate—
Himself was the Gate whereby men can
Enter the temple of God in man.

His words were shed softer than leaves from the pine,
And they fell on Sir Launfal as snows on the brine,
That mingle their softness and quiet in one
With a shaggy unrest they float down upon;
And a voice that was softer than silence said,
"Lo it is I, be not afraid!

"In many climes, without avail,
Thou hast spent thy life for the Holy Grail;
Behold it is here—this cup which thou
Didst fill at the streamlet for Me but now;
This crust is my body broken for thee,
This water His blood who died on the tree;

"The Holy Supper is kept, indeed,
In whatso we share with another's need;
Not what we give, but what we share—
For the gift without the giver is bare;
Who gives himself with his alms feeds three—
Himself, his hungering neighbor, and Me."

Sir Launfal woke as from a swound:
"The Grail in my castle here is found!
Hang my idle armor up on the wall;
Let it be the spider's banquet hall.

He must be fenced with stronger mail
Who would seek and find the Holy Grail."

The castle gate stands open now,
And the wanderer is as welcome to the hall
As the hangbird is to the elm-tree bough.
No longer scowl the turrets tall;
The summer's long siege at last is o'er.
When the first poor outcast went in at the door,
She entered with him in disguise,
And mastered the fortress by surprise.
There is no spot she loves so well on ground;
She lingers and smiles there the whole year round;

The meanest serf on Sir Launfal's land
Has hall and bower at his command;
And there's no poor man in the North Countree
But is Lord of the earldom as much as he.

We may not have all of the things for which Sir Launfal
sought, but we too have the same great privileges of making the
search; and it is written that only he who fails to seek, fails to
find.

The Miracles of Christmas

THE DICTIONARY SAYS that a miracle is an accomplishment that lies beyond human capability. We usually think of miracles as deviations from the laws of nature as we know them. The first miracle in the ministry of Jesus took place at Cana, when he turned the water into wine. When other people produced wine, they planted the vine and cared for the fruit until the grapes were ripe and ready for the wine press, but greater intelligence enabled Jesus to bring these elements together in quicker order.

He did many even more wonderful things. He made the blind to see, the lame to walk, and restored the dead to life. At age twelve he taught the wise men in the temple. He fed the multitude with five loaves and two fishes. He taught principles of righteousness, which, if followed, would not only make the people of our present world successful and happy but would also save our souls. One of the most significant miracles of Jesus took place when he broke the bands of death and initiated the universal bodily resurrection.

With justifiable pride we refer to that part of our knowledge explosion which took place on July 20, 1969, when we landed two American citizens upon the face of the moon. This event was hailed by one great American as the greatest event that has ever taken place since the Creation. Certainly it is no small thing to have two mortal men travel through space to reach another heavenly body, but this 24 billion dollar American miracle that enabled Mr. Armstrong and Mr. Aldrin to spend two hours and fourteen minutes on the moon pales into insignificance when compared to the fact that the Son of God spent some thirty-three years upon our earth.

From the time of the miraculous immaculate conception until he arose from the dead, his life was surrounded with miracles. Even the space travel of that first Christmas far surpasses our present abilities in that field. The important pre-Christmas wonders began to take place when an angel appeared to Zacharias and told him that he was to become the father of John the Baptist, who would be the Lord's forerunner. A few months later the same angel, Gabriel, was sent to a young woman in the city of Nazareth by the name of Mary and told her she was to bear the Son of God. (Luke 1:35.)

The understanding of this one fact alone, that Jesus Christ was and is the literal Son of God, has already worked untold miracles in the lives of many people. To be worthy of God's presence would be far more exciting than any trip to the moon could possibly be. In our age of wonders it took 24 billion dollars and many years of work by our greatest scientists to put two men on the moon, and even then they had to take with them the very air that they breathed. A whole multitude of heavenly beings came a much greater distance to sing heavenly anthems to the new-born king, and they came without the benefit of flying machines or space suits.

What a wonderful good fortune for us that, out of all of the planets in the vast domains of God, our earth should be honored by having the Son of God born here! Not only was he born upon the earth, but he came here in his official capacity as the world's Savior. He had been appointed in the grand council of heaven many years previously to be the Redeemer of all the earth's inhabitants on condition of their obedience. It is also significant that God's Only Begotten Son in the flesh was like us in form and appearance, and we know that he was also like God, his Eternal Father.

A divine revelation says that "God has created worlds without number," and he has peopled them with his own children, but his first begotten and most capable Son in the spirit who assisted God in these creations was ordained to be our Savior, example, and Redeemer.

The poet said:

> There was no other good enough
> To pay the price of sin.
> He only could unlock the gates
> Of heaven and let us in.

One of the greatest Christmas presents that we can conceive is that he has atoned for our sins on condition of our obedience. It should also substantially raise the value of our earth in our eyes to know that his own future as its Redeemer is also connected with it. We think of our earth as a pretty good place just as it is, but since the fall of Adam it has existed in its telestial or fallen state.

The Lord has told us many things about the glorious future of our earth. The time will soon come when the Son of God will again come to the earth. This time he will be accompanied by his mighty angels, and they will come in flaming fire to cleanse the earth and to inaugurate his millennial reign of a thousand years upon it. Then we will all know firsthand much more about peace and goodwill of which the angels sang on that first Christmas night so long ago. When he comes to rule, our earth will be raised in its status and will become a terrestrial earth. Then the paradisiacal beauty of its Garden of Eden days will be restored. The earth will then become a celestial sphere, and those who qualify for the celestial order of God will live upon it forever. If our earth is good enough that the Son of God should want to live here, then it must be pretty good, and certainly we should make the most of our own opportunity to live here eternally.

The greatest gift that we could give ourselves at Christmas time might be our own list of all the Christmas miracles we are the beneficiaries of. Of course, we still regret that there was no room found in the inn where he could be born, but it will be a much greater tragedy if there is no room for us on our celestialized earth because we have made no room in our lives for his love, his righteousness, and his obedience.

At Christmastime we love to think about the great new star that guided the wise men across the desert and enabled them to lay their treasures at the feet of the Prince of Peace and the King of kings. His life was also intended to be our guide, and the great scriptures were likewise given for that purpose.

In the same chapter in which Luke tells of the visit of the angels from heaven, he also tells of the earth growth made by Jesus as our example. Luke says: "And Jesus increased in wisdom and stature, and in favour with God and man." (Luke 2:52.) He increased in wisdom, which represents his great mental developments. He increased in stature, indicating his magnificent physical growth. He increased in his favor with God, which represents an important religious development, and he increased in his favor with man, which signifies his outstanding social progress. This fourfold program should also be a constant inspiration for us to follow.

Among the greatest of the miracles are the miracles of growth. By some mysterious process acorns can become oak trees. We get many wonders out of seeds. Human foreheads can grow broader, hearts can get bigger, vision can become more perceptive, spirituality can become more intense, and righteousness can become more all inclusive. God has made it possible that a thousand giant redwoods can come from an ounce of redwood seed, but the Creator's most serious concern was not about the welfare of redwoods. He was far more interested in having his offspring develop to become like their eternal parents.

One of the greatest Christmas thoughts is that we are the children of God formed in his image and in possession of his potentialities. Jesus grew up without sin unto salvation and then said: "Follow me." He organized his church upon the earth and indicated that we should belong to it. He taught the great principles of truth and outlined the means by which our eternal exaltation could be brought about. In giving the apostles their final instructions before his ascension, he said: "Go ye therefore, and teach all nations, baptising them in the name of the Father, and of the Son, and of the Holy Ghost: Teaching them to observe all things whatsoever I have commanded you: and, lo, I am with you alway, even unto the end of the world." (Matthew 28:19-20.)

Jesus announced his own interest in us by saying: ". . . I am come that they might have life, and that they might have it more abundantly." (John 10:10.) To increase the abundance of our lives is also one of the greatest of our own opportunities. We can get a good start in the right direction by getting the miracles of Christmas into our lives. Obedience to God is one of the wonder drugs of the spirit to increase our faith and vitalize our industry. We make some of our most dramatic and profitable responses to life at Christmastime.

Former President Hadley of Yale University once said: "The most important thing that anyone ever gets out of college is the college spirit." Then one begins to play for the school. Then his teammates become his brothers, and their success becomes quite as important to him as his own. It is likely that one of the most important things we can get out of Christmas is the spirit of Christ growing in our hearts. That is the spirit of "peace on earth, good will toward men." It is that spirit of love and righteousness that re-performs the miracles of Christmas in us. May we take full advantage of his wonderful Christmas miracles.

Lest We Forget

ONE OF THE great national rulers of our world was the British Queen Victoria. A crown was placed upon her head when she was just a girl in her teens. But she did her job very successfully, and during her long reign, ending at her death in 1901, England became the greatest nation that had ever existed upon our earth. Victoria ruled a territory which included over 25 per cent of all of the earth's surface. Her navies ruled the seven seas, and the sun never set on the British Empire.

One of the important events occurring during her rule was her Diamond Jubilee. This was a giant national demonstration that marked the sixtieth year of the notable reign of this great Christian queen. In commemorating the Jubilee, the *London Times* asked Rudyard Kipling to write an appropriate Jubilee poem. And the result was his famous "Recessional." The dictionary says that a recessional is something that marks a recession or a retreat. It is a song played at the end of a play while the audience is leaving. It is a hymn sung as the clergy and the choir are retiring from the chancel to the robing room. And Rudyard Kipling had some ideas about another kind of recessional.

In order to appreciate this poem, we might try to picture the pomp and pageantry of this great Jubilee of 1897 when England was at the height of her power. To this magnificent celebration came native princes from the Far East and ambassadors from the royal houses of Europe. There were vast military and naval displays, and a tremendous civic celebration with great processions, public services, and bonfires, all united to pour out a nation's adulation and praise to England's greatest queen.

To Mr. Kipling, a great empire in its dream of pride and power had seemed to lose sight of the great King of kings. And as the armies returned to their posts, the navies departed for their far-away island possessions, the kings and oriental chiefs returned, and the bonfires and jubilation died away, he pointed out their similarity to some of the other great nations of the past. His recessional was intended to recall the nation from its dream of pride and power, and the refrain of the poet became the prayer of the people. Within a few months after its publication, this great poem became one of the most widely known and admired in the language, and it is still appropriate to us for many reasons.

On one occasion Victoria was asked the reason why England had so far excelled all other nations of the earth. She laid her hand upon the Bible and said, "England is the land of the Book," and for a long time so it was. And as long as England lived by the precepts of the holy scriptures, her greatness continued to accelerate. But just as celebrations sometimes come to an end, so greatness and faith can also go into a recession or a retreat. And seventy-six years after Victoria's jubilee Rudyard Kipling might still be saying to us:

> God of our fathers, known of old,
>   Lord of our far-flung battleline,
> Beneath whose awful hand we hold
>   Dominion over palm and pine,
> Lord God of Hosts, be with us yet,
>   Lest we forget, Lest we forget!
>
> The tumult and the shouting dies,
>   The captains and the kings depårt;
> Still stands thine ancient sacrifice,
>   An humble and a contrite heart,
> Lord God of Hosts, be with us yet,
>   Lest we forget, Lest we forget!
>
> Far-called, our navies melt away,
>   On dune and headland sinks the fire,
> Lo, all our pomp of yesterday
>   Is one with Nineveh and Tyre!
> Judge of the nations, spare us yet,
>   Lest we forget, Lest we forget!
>
> If, drunk with sight of power, we loose
>   Wild tongues that have not thee in awe—
> Such boasting as the gentiles use
>   Or lesser breeds without the law—
> Lord god of hosts, be with us yet,
>   Lest we forget, Lest we forget!

For heathen heart that puts her trust
   In reeking tube and iron shard—
All valiant dust that builds on dust,
   And guarding, calls not thee to guard—
For frantic boast and foolish word,
   Thy mercy on thy people, Lord!
Amen.

It is interesting to try to remember that as a usual thing, when the speechmaking is over, when the honors have been conferred and the celebration has been finished, then is the time when the real work should actually begin.

And Rudyard Kipling's poem still has a great religious, as well as human, significance. It recalls when similar ambitions may have been celebrated in the ancient kingdoms of Nineveh and Tyre, which had long since destroyed themselves because they had forgotten God. They had also forgotten the contents of their own speeches and proclamations made in the days of their own power when they had celebrated their own greatness with festivities and military fanfare. Many of us also become drunk with our own importance and the possibilities of our own power, and we loose wild tongues that belie the rulership of God and the purpose of our own lives.

We are reminded of the interesting fact that some thirty-five centuries before Victoria, the Lord God of Hosts himself gathered the children of Israel together at the foot of Mount Sinai to make a covenant with them which, if they would keep it, would make them the greatest nation upon the earth. Then God came down onto the mount in a cloud of fire with such great power that the mountains shook and the people trembled. And then, to the accompaniment of the lightnings and thunders of Sinai, God gave the people that great set of laws by which true greatness could be won and maintained by them.

But after the commandments had been given, God also returned to his station. The fires died out on the mount. The lightning and thunders ceased. In Mr. Kipling's words, "the tumult and the shouting died," and the people were disbursed to continue their journey toward their promised land. It was also true for them that when the excitement was past, this was exactly the time for them to begin taking action.

Among other things, the Lord had said, "Remember the sabbath day, to keep it holy." He also wanted them to remember to do all of the other things that he had talked to them about. But unfortunately the people forgot many of these things. When the tumult and the shouting was over, many of the people went back to their golden calves and their other sins. If they had kept running through their minds Mr. Kipling's refrain of "Lord God of hosts, be with us yet lest we forget, lest we forget," they would not have been kept wandering in the wilderness for forty years until all except two of the original company over twenty years old had been denied their objectives and had perished in the wilderness. During this forty years and after the Israelites had many recessions in their faith when they should have been on fire with good works, they were often idle.

This idea of preventing any kind of a recession in our virtue or retreat in our enthusiasm and our faith is a very good one that we ourselves ought to work on. We have many periods during the year when we reach some kind of a high point. For example, someone has said that our civilization would never have survived for half a century if it had not been for this one day in seven that we call Sunday. After we have laid aside the cares that usually concern us during the other six days, we go to the house of prayer and let our minds reach upward while we try to understand the things of God. We may have a recession during the week days, but come again the Sabbath and we usually try to be back to our high point. And after the Sabbath is over is actually the time for us to advance to new levels instead of receding. Sunday should be a resting time when we prepare ourselves for greater accomplishments.

Then as the end of the year approaches we come to a kind of a Jubilee of the year in which we celebrate the Christmastime. This is the occasion when we commemorate the greatest event that ever took place upon this earth. This is when the Son of God came to our earth to establish his church to be our guide in conduct and faith. The results of our obedience to his laws determines our own eternal success.

And as the children of Israel made great preparations for their festivities of thirty-five centuries ago, and as the British made great preparations for their celebration of 1897,* so each year as the Christmas season approaches, we prepare our homes,

* Victoria's Jubilee.

sing our Christmas hymns, say our Christmas prayers, read our Christmas literature, and preach our Christmas sermons.

Then, as the old year comes to its close, we repack the tinsel and the ornaments; we throw out the Christmas tree and take down the colored lights. The Christmas carols are taken off the radio and our Christmas sermons are no longer heard in our churches. Sometimes we also forget the purpose of the divine birth in Bethlehem as well, and those significant doctrines for which his life stood. However, instead of conducting a retreat from the high points of Christmas, we might get into our minds some antidotes to prevent us from going into a recession. Then we might sing with Mr. Kipling, "Lord God of hosts, be with us yet, lest we forget, lest we forget!"

At that point in our year where the Christmas season ends and the New Year begins is a traditional time when we make our New Year's resolutions, and we might control those wild tongues and contrary deeds that are active when we get drunk with the temptations to retreat from the high thoughts centered around the birth, life, and death of the Savior of the world. Actually, when the Christmas celebrations are over and we are filled with the Spirit of him whose birth we celebrate, that is the time when the real work of Christmas should actually begin. For with our lives, as with our marriages and as with our Christmas celebrations, we are judged more by our works than by the most beautiful Christmas anthems that come out of our hearts. And here is a great Christmas idea which says:

When the song of the angels is heard no more,
When the Bethlehem star has gone from the sky,
When the kings and the wise men have returned to their homes,
When the shepherds are back in the fields with their flocks,
Then the real work of Christmas should eagerly begin,
To spread the Christian message,
To lift up the unbelieving,
To make whole the broken hearted,
To break the bonds of sin,
To purify the national purpose,
To exalt the destiny of all mankind,
And to set our eyes on those eternal goals
That the son of God established in his day.

There are many Christmas carols, songs of thanksgiving, and hymns of praise and worship that are appropriate throughout the entire year. There are also some great hymns of jubilation that we might sing while we are waiting for the high point of Christmas to come again. One of these is Mr. Kipling's great poem "Lest We Forget." Another inspiring jubilee prayer was written by Daniel C. Roberts, entitled "God of Our Fathers," which was set to music by G. W. Warren. Mr. Roberts says:

> God of our fathers, Whose almighty hand
> Leads forth in beauty all the starry band
> Of shining words in splendor through the skies,
> Our grateful songs before thy throne arise.
>
> Thy love divine hath led us in the past;
> In this free land by thee our lot is cast;
> Be thou our Ruler, Guardian, Guide, and Stay,
> Thy word our law, thy paths our chosen way.
>
> From war's alarms, from deadly pestilence,
> Be thy strong arm our ever sure defense;
> Thy true religion in our hearts increase,
> Thy bounteous goodness nourish us in peace.

Someday the festivities of our lives themselves will also come to an end. Our activities will be over; the fires of our life will have died down. Then the real work of life will be about ready to begin. It has been said that death is not our final sleep, it is our eternal awakening. Death is the key that unlocks the mansions of eternity. Then will be the time for the great blessings that we sang about to be realized. And in the meantime may God help us to live by the book that we may begin our immortal lives with no depressions or recessionals, so that we may pray, "Lord God of hosts, be with us yet, lest we forget, lest we forget!"

Index